NEW APPROACHES TO THE EUCHARIST

New Approaches to the Eucharist

Colman O'Neill, O.P.

Nihil Obstat:

M.-St. Morard, O.P., S.T.M.

V. M. Kuiper, O.P., S.T.M.

Imprimi Potest:

Th. E. Mehrle, O.P., S.T.M., Superior

Imprimatur:

† Th. Perroud, Vicar General

Fribourg, Switzerland - December 12, 1966

Library of Congress Catalog Number: 67 - 24921

Designed, printed and bound in the U.S.A. by the Pauline Fathers and Brothers of the Society of St. Paul at Staten Island, New York as a part of their communications apostolate.

CONTENTS

1

THE DEBATE ON THE EUCHARIST

The fact that the doctrine of the Eucharist is being subjected to a new and searching theological analysis was brought before the notice of the Church by the publication of the papal encyclical, *Mysterium fidei,* towards the end of 1965.[1] On its appearance the encyclical aroused in certain quarters considerable unfavorable comment, being greeted, in fact, with a degree of passionate disapproval which must be rare for such a document.[2]

The general public was not without forewarning that certain new positions were being adopted within the Church on the

---

1. The encyclical is dated: September 3, 1965; cf. *Acta Apostolicae Sedis,* 57 (1965), 753-774; English translation: *Doctrine and Life* (Dublin), 15 (1965), 572-575, 639-645; 16 (1966), 45-55; other English translations are available.

2. The encyclical was published a few days before the opening of the final session of the Council, which may account for the somewhat tense atmosphere in which it was received. A typical unfavorable reaction may be found in an editorial of *Commonweal,* September 4, 1965, which was followed by a restatement of position. Ibid., October 15, 1965.

Eucharist.[3] It may perhaps be doubted, however, whether the true state of the problem was widely grasped either before or after the issuance of the encyclical.

In spite of the somewhat exaggerated complaints with which the encyclical was in some places greeted, the document itself turns out, on careful reading, to be a conscious attempt at finding an orthodox equilibrium between apparently opposed views of the Eucharist. This does not prevent a firm stand being taken on what the Church understands the Eucharist to be. Nor does it prevent the inclusion of a very specific statement on the permanent value of the theological terms used in dogmatic formulas and of the concepts which these terms express.

With this last factor the limited field of the Eucharist is left behind; it is the nature of the whole task of theology within the Church which is brought into discussion. For one of the tasks which modern theologians have set themselves is the restatement of revelation in terms which are meaningful to contemporary man. The encyclical, written as it was in the context of a Council of renewal, could scarcely fail to be sympathetic to this forbidding undertaking. Yet, for all its undoubted sympathy, it marks out, or seems to, a very clearly-defined area within which such an undertaking may legitimately be carried on.

In these wider perspectives the question is one of the extent to which the Church can admit new interpretations of her traditional teaching which are formulated in the categories of contemporary philosophies. It is not sufficient for one party to this debate to dismiss as uninformed conservatism the reluctance of many Catholic theologians to admit such new interpretations. Nor is it sufficient, on the other hand, for the other party to accuse of philosophical immaturity those who attempt new interpretation. Such sweeping judgments are, perhaps, understandable if not excusable; for it is an extraordinarily difficult thing for one who holds deep convictions concerning philosophical or theological method to view with sympathy and true understanding a contrary opinion. Yet, beyond this clash of deep-seated intellectual attitudes, there lies, and remains, the perennial Christian question of the relationship between revelation and reason, between the word of God and the response of man.

If the word of God is, in itself, a divine act of grace for man, it is, nevertheless, a word which, by the nature of the event, has become immanent in humanity. Here, for all its saving power, it is at the mercy of human understanding. Because of its power it may still, in spite of misinterpretations, recreate men in the likeness of Christ. Yet the task of theology within the Church is to formulate a human understanding of the word of God. To appeal to the mystery of the word in order to justify divergent or even contradictory human interpretations of it is to fail to realize that the word has truly become immanent in mankind—and this without prejudice to its transcendence. To speak of the immanence of the word is to proclaim the dignity of man, made in the image of God. The Word of God, in whom all things were made, does not call for the sacrifice of the human intellect. Any word that renders man's reason irrelevant is not the word of God. It matters what man thinks about revelation.

That all human interpretations will be incomplete follows directly from the transcendence of the Word: it is spoken by God, the One who, while being the ground of being, is wholly other. It follows, too, that the theologian must always be vigilant to complement his own interpretation by that of others. Here a true community of human effort is not only possible, but necessary. Yet, just at this level of human effort, some interpretations are, at least in part, mutually exclusive.

A recognition of one's own limitations will certainly suggest dialogue when the lines of such a clash have been clearly drawn.

---

3. *Time* magazine had reported on recent discussions in the issue of July 2, 1965. There had also been an inconclusive exchange of letters in *The Tablet* (London), February 3, 13, 20, 27, and March 6, 1965.

There is, however, a third party to such a dialogue; or perhaps it would be better to say that the two parties are united in a higher personality, that of the Church, with the teaching authority granted by Christ to his Church. And, while interventions by the teaching authority cannot realistically be supposed to solve human dilemmas, they can at least draw more firmly the lines of discussion.

The teaching authority too is clearly conditioned by historical circumstances; and its interventions may at times appear, or be, inadequate or out of touch with the theological dialogue. The dialogue is not, consequently, suppressed and theologians are left to strive for sympathetic understanding of each other's views as the only means by which their common task may be furthered. The immanence of the word requires this. But in this the teaching authority may not be ignored as irrelevant. It always introduces a positive element into the discussion, even though it may be left to theologians to debate on the particular relevance of this element.

It is, then, to a specifically human task that the theologian sets himself: that of being human about God. The limitations attendant upon the results of such a task are obvious. Yet to renounce the task, or to refuse to pursue it relentlessly (by, for example, electing to content oneself with biblical theology), is less than human; and it seems certain that every Christian, consciously or unconsciously, in simple or in reflective fashion, sets himself to it. This is the justification for theological debate and for the disagreement which, no less than agreement, it engenders.

Without doubt it is significant that it is on the sacrament of the blessed Eucharist that the new theological controversy should be centred. Linked with our understanding of the Eucharist is our whole understanding of the Church as the body of Christ and, indeed, our understanding of the relationship between creation and redemption, between reason and faith, between the Christian and Christ. Does not Karl Barth say somewhere that to accept the Catholic doctrine of the Eucharist is to accept the Catholic Church?

Current discussion of the Eucharist is concerned both with the classical problem of the real presence and with the liturgical practice of the faithful. The practical problems—in particular the celebration of Mass without a congregation and the forms to be given to Eucharistic devotion—have been raised in the context of the conciliar reform of the liturgy. Yet they too, as much as the problem of transubstantiation, call into question the fundamental theological notions of the Eucharist and it is only if an attempt is made to see them in these perspectives that any valid Christian solution can be proposed to them.

The shape of the present discussions is in fact determined by the two basic problems of communitary participation and the real presence. The first concerns directly the Church, the second Christ's presence in the Church. The attitude one adopts to these two questions will determine the whole character of one's Eucharistic devotion. To these two problems the principal part of the following pages is devoted.

Another aspect of the liturgy at present under discussion is the relationship between the ministry of the word and the sacraments. Again, this is a theme brought into prominence by the Council. I shall consider this problem first for it will help us to locate the Eucharist in the life of the Church, and in particular it will establish the relationship between the ordained priesthood and the sacrament, an essential point for the discussion of the celebration of Mass.

2

WORD, SACRAMENT AND EUCHARIST

With increasing awareness of the fundamental role which the ministry of the word plays in the building up of the body of Christ in the Church, Catholic theologians are at present probing the relationship between this ministry and the sacraments. [1] The ecumenical interest of such an undertaking is clear. The significance of the question in determining the nature of the ordained priesthood has already been referred to. Now that the sacraments are seen more and more clearly to be an integral part of the ministry of the word, the implications for liturgical practice in the Church are being gradually brought to light. It is becoming clearer that the personal response of faith which is demanded of the hearer of the word is equally demanded of the recipient of the sacraments.

The traditional doctrine of the "dispositions" necessary for receiving a sacrament did make practical provision for the personal participation of the faithful in the sacraments. But it appears true to say that no explicit theological syn-

---

1. Cf., e.g., K. Rahner, "Wort und Eucharistie," in *Aktuelle Fragen zur Eucharistie,* ed. M. Schmaus, Munich, 1960; *Wort und Sakrament,* ed. H. Fries, Munich, 1966.

thesis was established in the context of this traditional teaching between the hearing of the word and the reception of the sacraments.

The Tridentine formula, attributing *ex-opere-operato* efficacy to the seven sacraments, undoubtedly contributed, as it was used by theologians, to intellectual rigidity. The formula was proffered in theological writings literally as a *deus ex machina* as an answer to problems concerning sacramental efficacy; whereas, in fact, it poses a question. For, if the problem of the Christian life is taken seriously, how is it possible to maintain that the sacraments possess an efficacy which is, in some fashion, conceived as being independent of the moral effort of the recipient? [2]

WORD AND SACRAMENT

If the sacraments are to be correlated with the ministry of the word it is necessary to go beyond the narrow connotation of "word" as teaching or preaching. The common origin of both ministries of the Church must be sought in the creative and redemptive word of God himself. This is an efficacious word, one which realizes its content simply because it is spoken.

But the word of God, in its effects, becomes immanent in the world; and here it takes many forms. If it will be fully articulated only in the eschatological union of mankind with God in Christ, its efficacy may already be discerned in the world and in the mystery of Christ which is being realized in the world. If we consider this immanent word only in its re-creative or redemptive efficacy (leaving aside, therefore, the presupposed word of creation), then it appears in two-fold form. There are first the words the men speak about God and about his design of salvation; and these words in their original form are inspired, constituting in the fullest sense the word of God immanent in humanity. There are also the actions of God in the world, in implementation of his saving design and these constitute the saving word of God immanent in the world. Through human word and saving action, the two forming an inner unity, God is revealed in the world, and in his revelation salvation is brought to men.

Without revelation through the spoken (or written) word man could not be saved. For he is a creature made in the image of God and enjoys personal freedom. His freedom extends to the word of God itself, which he may either accept or reject. Yet the word only clarifies and manifests God's action in the world, a saving action which is an act of grace, transcending man's power of choice, bestowing the gift of salvation. It is the word which humanizes the mystery of God's action, transposing it into the field of possibilities open to human decision.

It appears, then, false to attribute, without modification, to the words that men speak about God, even when they are inspired, the efficacy which properly belongs to the Word of God himself. The human word is an integral element in the realization of the mystery of the divine word of salvation; but it is inserted at the specifically human level of this mystery.

Only in the Word himself made flesh is this complementary duality of word and action transcended. In him the revelation of the divine design is brought to its fulfillment—in his words and in his actions "but especially through his death and glorious resurrection from the dead and final sending of the Spirit of truth." [3] At the heart of this revelation, and as part of it, is brought into the world the act of reconciliation by which divine salvation is actively realized among men. What Christ achieved in his sacrifice—which was manifested in its universal

---

2. Cf. C. O'Neill, *Meeting Christ in the Sacraments,* New York, 1964; Cork, 1966; pp. 137-160.

3. Vatican II, Dogmatic Constitution, *Dei Verbum,* on divine revelation, ch. 1, n. 4. See the whole chapter on the relation between word and action.

significance by his resurrection-ascension and by Pentecost—is salvation made over to men. His human word can communicate salvation at the same time as it appeals to human freedom.

It is Christ's work of reconciliation which gives the Church its character as the community of salvation. For the Church is primarily the community of those who approach God in virtue of the sacrifice of Christ; it is, in other words, in its deepest reality a priestly community, participating in the sacrifice of the high priest. It is the corporeal, social and historical manifestation of the sacrifice of the cross.

It is just because of this dependence on Christ's act of reconciliation that there is, within the priestly community of the Church, an order of priests representing Christ the head of the Church, and participating in the mission given to the apostles. It did, indeed, belong to the mission of the apostles to announce the Good News of salvation; and their words and the words of the Scriptures as they reveal the mystery of Christ are external signs of grace. Their words, and above all the words of the Scriptures, continue as the immanent, human, verbal expression of the divine Word made flesh; and, as such, they form an integral part of the realization of Christ's mystery among men, appealing, as all human words do, to man's freedom. But this was not the heart of the apostolic mission. What they bore witness to by their words was precisely that the Word was made flesh—and that, consequently, the divine saving action was now immanent in the humanity of Christ. By their words they pointed to the Word which is efficacious; and then it became apparent that this meant that at the heart of their ministry of the word the duality of word and saving action was transcended, as it was in Christ himself. They were not only witnesses; their witness reached a point of intensity where the One to whom they witnessed lent to their words an efficacy which belongs only to his word.

The Constitution on the Sacred Liturgy expresses as follows the two levels of intensity in the apostolic mission:

> Just as Christ was sent by the Father, so also he sent the apostles, filled with the Holy Spirit. This he did so that, by preaching the gospel to every creature (cf. Mk. 16: 15), they might proclaim that the Son of God, by his death and resurrection, had freed us from the power of Satan (cf. Acts 26: 18) and from death, and brought us into the kingdom of his Father. His purpose was also that they might exercise the work of salvation which they were proclaiming, by means of the sacrifice and sacraments, around which the entire liturgical life revolves. [4]

It was when they "exercised" the work of salvation that the apostles acted immediately in the person of the high priest, bringing his saving act of reconciliation into the community of the Church.

The human proclamation of the word attains a new intensity in the sacraments. Always, whether the ministry is that of preaching or that of the sacraments, it is the word which is being proclaimed. And this word can be received only by faith. When it is so received, the work of salvation is realized. Yet, at the heart of this mystery of the word, there are the sacraments which mean more than the human proclamation of Christ's saving deeds, because they contain more than the simple word.

What this "more" is can be best seen in the Mass. Here it is not merely the Good News of Christ's redemptive sacrifice that is *announced* to men. This element is present, as St. Paul's words in I Corinthians 11:26, interpreted in their most obvious sense, make clear. But the sacrifice—the unique sacrifice which is the subject of the Good News—is *itself* made

---

4. Vatican II, *Sacrosanctum Concilium,* ch. 1, n. 6.

present. This is to say that the very act of divine salvation in Christ, on which the Church essentially rests, is realized within the Church. It is unnecessary here to reiterate the common teaching that this re-presentation in no way prejudices the uniqueness of Christ's redeeming sacrifice. It is sufficient to say that the mystery of the Mass is located, not on the side of Christ's act of redemption, but on the side of the application of this act to his members.

What is important is the significance of this representation of Christ's unique sacrifice for the faith of the Church. Christ's central act of reconciliation is always the object of faith. But in the Mass faith has more to hold on than a mere word proclaiming Christ's deed. Here it has the sacrifice presented to it in a more integrally human fashion, so that the believer not merely holds by faith that his Christian life may be incorporated into Christ's sacrifice: the victim itself of this sacrifice lies on the altar, and this *reality* gives corporeal expression to inner union with Christ. This is more human because inner intentions are not adequately human until they become "incarnate" in bodily expression. This is more Christian because the humanization of faith in bodily expression is not merely symbolic; within the mystery of the mystical body, it is actual. The interior unity of the mystical body is expressed humanly in the one and only victim of the New Alliance.

A similar integrally human dimension is given to the meeting with Christ in the other sacraments. These are all set in the context of the proclamation of the word and continue it. But, because they come at decisive moments in the life of the Christian, they occasion a fuller commitment on the part of the Church, the sacrament of Christ. The word of salvation, efficacious only in so far as it is an integral element in the realization of salvation, reaches a new intensity. Always a sign of grace, it now shares immediately in the power of Christ's word, the efficacious word of God. In the sacramental word the word is uttered so that the unique act of reconciliation becomes effective for those who receive it in faith. Faith is not superseded; it remains the necessary response to the word. But the man who is held by faith finds in a fellow-man, who ministers to him, Christ himself, the Redeemer, in integrally bodily form.

It is not of importance here to attempt to justify the doctrine of *ex-opere-operato* efficacy. As will be said in a later chapter, this in no fashion implies that the Christian is dispensed from personal participation in the mystery of Christ. If the distinctive character of the sacraments is to be discovered within the context of the all-embracing ministry of the word, it must be sought in the fuller, and more integrally human, meeting with Christ which these liturgical actions make possible. The sacraments bring Christ into the Church through the word of his ministers *and* in a more fully bodily, though sacramental, form. The qualification "sacramental" must be added. For though the sacraments surpass the simple word in tending towards the bodily presence of Christ, they still remain, as far as normal human encounter is concerned, within the dimension of symbolism. It is only because of the presence of Christ within the symbols—a presence which is believed but is not dependent on the individual's belief—that the value of the symbols transcends what faith itself could achieve.

PRIESTLY APOSTOLATE AND SACRAMENT

If the word attains its most intense form in the sacraments it follows that it is in the sacraments too that the apostolic mission finds its deepest meaning. In the sacraments the office of the successors of the apostles finds its determining element. The bishop, who possesses the fulness of the priestly office, exercising by divine right the ministry of the word and ordering the administration of the sacraments, is primarily the minister of the Eucharist. For it is Christ himself who, through the minister of the Eucharist, forms his community on earth. In the order of the Christian mystery, it is at a moment subsequent to this that the community so formed by Christ himself is given to the pastoral care of the successors of the apostles. That evangelization must precede the administration of the sacraments is clear; and so the ministry of the word enjoys a temporal primacy. But this remains at the human level. Christ in the Eucharist anticipates his minister's words. Their preaching depends on his saving presence in the Church. [5]

The priest, who participates in the Christ-representative office of the bishop, does so directly in the latter's Eucharistic role. And it is because of this that he can be associated by the bishop with the episcopal pastoral charge. The essential element in the priest's ordination is the power given him to offer the Eucharistic sacrifice in the person of Christ the head, thus making this sacrifice available to all the members of Christ in the Church. Clearly, his activity would be less than priestly, in the integral sense, if his celebration of the Mass were not set in the context of the ministry of the word. It is only by means of the word that he can make the sacramental sacrifice meaningful for the Christian existence of the people. Yet, to preach the word, he must be formally adopted as a cooperator by a bishop. The priest's Eucharistic rôle already gives him hierarchical status adapting him for such episcopal adoption. It is, in other words, the Eucharist which provides the inner bond of union between the college of bishops and the college of presbyters.

This has an obvious application in the determination of the coordinating factor in specifically priestly (as distinguished from lay) "spirituality." If the layman is to be defined in terms of his secular task, [6] (which clearly has a reference to the Eucharist), the priest's life (and that of the bishop) is one which is immediately concerned with the Eucharist and, then, with seeking to establish the proximate conditions in which the Eucharist may suitably be celebrated. [7] It will be seen how closely allied is this view of the priestly life with the definition of the Church, given above, as the community of those who approach God through the sacrifice of Christ.

EUCHARIST

It is through the sacraments that the Church is truly the body of the incarnate Word. The humanity of the Word is present to the Church, not only through the ministry of the word—which would already be ecclesial incarnation—but also in actions which are assimilated to Christ's humanity, sharing in its power. On their side, the faithful are not confined to a not-fully-human encounter with Christ in his word; their meeting with him tends towards full human encounter when,

---

5. M. Schmaus, "Hirtenamt der Kirche," *Lexikon für Theologie und Kirche* (2nd ed.), V (1960), col. 386-7, also sees the power of Orders (the Eucharist) as more fundamental than the pastoral office (teaching and order). Other authors would disagree; but the opinion held on this matter appears to depend on the efficacy attributed to the ministry of the word. If the sacraments are seen as only another example of this ministry, then the word will be given priority. If, as I have argued, the sacraments transcend the ministry of the word, the Eucharistic power will be held to predominate. It is not unlikely that this difference of opinion has its roots in the old controversy regarding physical and moral causality of the sacraments.

6. Cf. Vatican II, Dogmatic Constitution, *Lumen Gentium,* on the Church, ch. 4, n. 31.

7. Cf. Vatican II, Decree, *Presbyterorum ordinis,* on the ministry and life of priests, ch. 2, n. 5 (cp. n. 4), n. 6; ch. 3, n. 13: "Priests fulfill their chief duty in the mystery of the Eucharistic Sacrifice. In it the work of our redemption continues to be carried out. For this reason, priests are strongly urged to celebrate Mass every day, for even if the faithful are unable to be present, it is an act of Christ and the Church." – This close association of the priest with the Eucharist, *futurae gloriae pignus,* is surely not without relevance to priestly celibacy, if marriage is explicitly a commitment to secular reality.

expressing their faith in community worship, they find him and the power of his humanity in other Christians.

It is in the Eucharist that this incarnational—that is to say, humanizing—movement approaches most closely to its ideal. The ideal is unobtainable before the return of Christ; but in this sacrament it might seem to be within grasp. Because Christ has not returned, because his work of reconciliation must still be communicated to his members, the Eucharist brings him into the Church in the state of victim. This is the form of union with him which is required by those who still await resurrection: they are to sacrifice with him, until sin has been finally conquered. Yet in Christ himself sin is already conquered, and it is only through him that this victory may become ours. It is as the risen Christ that he comes in the Eucharist, communicating the Spirit of charity: for our sacrifice, taking the form of victim; in himself, risen and glorious. These are the two aspects of the Eucharist. In both it is Christ himself who comes to us, in his humanity.

The word must be silent in the presence of the Word; and yet the word spoken at the consecration still lingers. It must still be received in faith if the presence of the Word is to be discovered, for the presence of his humanity is still mediated; it is not immediately perceptible. But what faith recognizes here is not just the word of Christ; it knows that it is Christ himself among us.

This is the heart of the Church. The Constitution on the Liturgy refers to the Eucharist as the principal reason why the liturgy "is the summit toward which the activity of the Church is directed . . . the fountain from which all her power flows." [8] Variations on this theme occur again and again in the Conciliar documents. [9] The fullest explanation of it is found in the Decree, *Presbyterorum ordinis,* on the ministry and life of priests:

The other sacraments, as well as all ecclesial ministries and

> apostolic undertakings, are linked with the blessed Eucharist and directed towards it. For contained in the blessed Eucharist is the entire spiritual good of the Church [cf. St. Thomas, *Summa theol.* III, q. 65, a. 3, ad 1; q. 79, a. 1, c. and ad 1], that is to say, Christ himself, he who is our Pasch and the living bread, he who through his flesh—vivified and rendered life-giving by the Holy Spirit—gives life to men. In this fashion they are called upon and brought to offer, in union with him, themselves, their work, the whole of creation. From this it may be seen that the Eucharist is the source and summit of all evangelization; for, while catechumens are introduced progressively to participation in the sacrament, the faithful, already sealed by baptism and confirmation, are integrally inserted into the body of Christ by reception of the Eucharist. [10]

It is in similar but briefer terms that the encyclical, *Mysterium fidei* accounts for the Council's repeated concern to promote active, integral participation in the Eucharistic mysteries: this sacrament is "the fount of life which cleanses and strengthens us so that we live, not for ourselves but for God and are bound together by the closest bonds of love." [11]

---

8. Vatican II, *Sacrosanctum Concilium,* ch. 1, n. 10.

9. Cf. Dogmatic Constitution, *Lumen gentium,* on the Church, ch. 2, n. 11; ch. 3, nn. 26, 28; ch. 4, n. 33; ch. 7, n. 50; Decree, *Presbyterorum ordinis,* on the ministry and life of priests, ch. 2, nn. 5, 6; ch. 3, n. 14; Decree, *Ad gentes,* on the missionary activity of the Church, ch. 6, n. 39; Decree *Unitatis redintegratio,* on ecumenism, ch. 3, n. 15; Decree, *Apostolicam actuositatem,* on the apostolate of the laity, ch. 1, n. 3; Decree, *Christus Dominus,* on the pastoral office of bishops in the Church, ch. 2, n. 30; Decree *Perfectae caritatis,* on the apt renewal of religious life, nn. 6, 15; Decree, *Optatam totius Ecclesiae renovationem,* on the formation of priests, nn. 4, 8.

10. Ch. 2, n. 5 (in square brackets, footnote in the conciliar text).

11. § 3 (*Acta Ap. Sed.,* loc. cit. [cf. note 1, above], 754).

3

THE MASS: COMMUNITARY AND PRIVATE CELEBRATION

That doubts have arisen about the legitimacy of privately-celebrated Masses is one of the points of concern noted by Paul VI in his review of current tendencies in Eucharistic theology and practice in the encyclical *Mysterium fidei.* He points out that misunderstanding of the Council's liturgical reform, with its stress on communal participation, is the source of the unrest. To this may be added the opinions of some theologians which may possibly have been interpreted as lending doctrinal support to these doubts.

The unrest, arising from the practical liturgical modifications introduced by the Council, has manifested itself among many who are directly responsible for the instruction of the faithful and especially among many of the younger clergy. Some of those affected will argue that privately-celebrated Masses are of comparatively late origin in the Church (8th-9th cent.) and can be linked with the introduction of Mass stipends. But such arguments, while they raise genuine questions, are only secondary, even in the minds of their proponents. It is, in any case, difficult to see how a long-standing, approved Church practice can be discarded on the grounds stated.

More significant, because of more profound psychological relevance, would appear to be the influence of the liturgical reform itself. In the case of many dedicated pastors it is unfortunate that their understanding of the reform lacked theological depth, being almost entirely shaped by the immediate demands of achieving a considerable change in the people's way of worship, and of providing the necessary instruction and encouragement which this change demands. This is, undoubtedly, no more than a phenomenon of a time of transition; and the interest shown by the clergy in the theological background to the reform will ensure that the time for expedients is not unduly prolonged.

With the younger clergy there is the added difficulty of an abrupt change from the highly-developed communal liturgy of the seminary to the less ideal conditions of a parish or small religious house. In the nature of things the problem of Mass without a congregation is more likely to be a difficulty that the young priest of a religious order has to confront, and it can only be heightened by the growing practice of concelebration to which he is becoming accustomed in his seminary.

In the light of these difficulties, and in order to provide a background for the discussion of the theological problems referred to, it will be helpful to consider the meaning of the communal celebration of the Mass before going on to the problem of private celebration.

The sacrificial character of the Mass will be taken for granted. It is worth while noting, however, that *Mysterium fidei* refers to this as "the synthesis and principal point" of the doctrine of the Eucharist since, as the Council of Trent expressed it, through this mystery the sacrifice of the cross is represented, continually brought to mind, and its saving power applied for the remission of our daily sins. [1]

This doctrine of the sacrifice already foreshadows the teaching on the real presence. For if in the Mass the sacramental body and blood of Christ are truly offered as the victim of the sacrifice, then any theory which postulates a merely "dynamic" presence of Christ must be judged inadequate. Conceivably, if the Mass liturgy were simply a communion service, a presence of Christ "for us"—in the manner in which he is present in the other sacraments—would be sufficient to account for the union of charity which is promoted by the Eucharist. But if, as Catholic teaching holds, Christ is truly offered in a sacramental sacrifice, then a more "real" or "substantial" presence is called for in the Eucharist than that which is granted the Church in the other sacraments.

I: COMMUNAL CELEBRATION

MASS AND THE CHURCH

What we must look for is the link between the Mass-sacrifice and the mystery of the Church. This, when found, will provide a key to the liturgical reform and at the same time justify Masses celebrated without a congregation. On a superficial showing, it might well appear contradictory that two forms of liturgical celebration, so radically different from one another, should rest on a single point of doctrine. Yet authentic understanding of the Mass-liturgy begins with the resolution of precisely this paradox.

The doctrine of the Mass throws light on the mystery of the Church; and what we know of the Church illumines the mystery of the Mass. The Mass is the supreme action of the Church, so that the structure of the Church, known from revelation as the body of Christ, manifests itself in the Mass. The community of the faithful in Christ is reflected in the Mass.

---

1. *Mysterium fidei,* § 27 (*Acta Ap. Sed.*, 57 [1965], 759; cf. ch. 1, n. 1).

This means, first of all, that "the Church, fulfilling in union with Christ the role of priest and victim, as a whole offers the sacrifice of the Mass and in this is itself, as a whole, offered.[2] This point will be more thoroughly discussed later.

Secondly, the reflection of the structure of the Church in the Mass means that the mystery of the Church is not being seen in all its divine and human fulness if liturgical participation is reduced to the newly-introduced form of congregational participation—however much this reform itself, in its turn, illumines the mystery of the Church. Liturgical participation is simply a moment in the life of the Church, and reveals, consequently, the structure of the Church. It is visible and sacramental; and at the same time, it is a mystery of grace.

ACTIVE PARTICIPATION

Basic to the thought that the whole Church offers the Mass is the principle of cooperation between Christ and his members. This principle would still be valid even if doubts were to be raised as to whether the *whole* Church is truly involved in each Mass. The communal Mass of a particular congregation is, in any case, the outcome of an application of the principle.[3] For this reason, a word of explanation of the principle is needed.

It must first be grasped that the whole life of the Church lies in the sphere of the mystery of the risen Christ. This seems fairly obvious when we speak simply of the Church, and should be just as obvious when we speak explicitly of that action of the Church which is the sacrifice of the Mass. Perhaps it is the notion of "sacrifice" which leads to confusion; for this seems to hark back to man's pre-redeemed state, before the all-sufficient sacrifice of Christ. By explicitly locating the Mass-sacrifice in the mystery of the risen Christ we leave no doubt that this sacrifice is dependent on the unique sacrifice of Christ and is derived from the gift of the Spirit sent into the world by the Christ ascended to his Father and established *Son of God in power* (Romans 1:4). It is within the sphere of this communication of Christ's paschal mystery that there is a sacramental representation of the unique sacrifice. And such a sacramental dimension is given this unique sacrifice in order that the faithful, who have not yet risen, not yet received the full fruits of redemption, may participate in the sacrifice. If the mystery of Christ is manifested on earth in the sacrament of the Church, this extends to his sacrifice.

There is a close connection between this teaching and the Catholic doctrine of justification; and it is here that the sense of the principle of cooperation becomes clear. Because the Church believes that the faithful are *interiorly* transformed by grace (and in this *personal* way have the justice of Christ imputed to them), she consequently teaches that they can, always under and with Christ, cooperate freely and responsibly in their own salvation. This is a work of grace (that is, given by God); it is brought about, therefore, by the cross of Christ. Yet it is accomplished in such a way that it enables the Christian personally and actively to share in the unique and fundamental act of Christian atonement and worship which took place on Calvary.

Here lies the central reality of the common priesthood of the baptized. It consists in a union with, and active sharing in, the worship, obedience and love which inspired Christ

---

2. Encyc., *Mysterium fidei,* § 31 (*Acta Ap. Sed.,* loc. cit., 761). The teaching clearly reflects that of the Council, particularly of the Constitution on the Church. To my knowledge, however, nowhere does the Council use the expression: "the Church *as a whole,*" used twice in the encyclical.

3. The principle is appealed to in the Constitution on Sacred Liturgy (*Sacrosanctum Concilium*), ch. 1, n. 7: "Christ indeed always associates the Church with himself in the truly great work of giving perfect praise to God and making men holy."

throughout his earthly existence, but especially on the cross, and which are still his in heaven.

What is here called the central reality of the common priesthood is based on *faith* in Christ. But in so far as it also derives from *baptism* this priesthood is lived in the context of the visible Church, finding in the actions of the Church its full and normal development.

It may not be out of place to analyze the notion of the common priesthood. For the sake of clarity of explanation, the two bases of the common priesthood—faith and baptism (with confirmation)—have been distinguished. This evidently involves introducing distinctions into what is, in liturgical activity, an existential unity. A similar "split-level" approach is commonly adopted to the objective reality of the Church with its inner, eschatological mystery of grace and its visible, historical activity. In the individual member and in the community, however, these two elements contribute, as complementary principles, to a single activity. The action proceeding from sanctifying grace is concretely always sacramentalized, that is, directed towards, expressed in, and relevant for, an external action of the visible Church. So, for example, the secular activity of the confirmed Christian is an authentic action of the Church, just as his life of grace is expressed in the Mass and in the sacraments he receives. The purpose of drawing attention to the distinction between faith and baptism is not, then, to introduce some sort of inhuman dichotomy into the active liturgical participation of the faithful. Nor is it meant to legitimize willful disregard of the Council's clear desire for integral active participation in the liturgy. But, because the distinction is based on the nature of the Church, it permits a judgment on the relative significance and values of the various elements which go to make up this form of participation. Such a judgment, in its turn, makes possible a realistic appraisal of what is pastorally desirable, in any given circumstances, in the matter of active participation. Clearly, in an appraisal of this sort, the judgment of the Council concerning the general circumstances of the Church at the present time will play a preponderant role. It still remains that local conditions may be exceptional; and then the local liturgical authority, normally the bishop, is at liberty to introduce whatever modifications he considers within the general framework of the conciliar constitution.

At Mass the ecclesial dimension of the common priesthood reaches its climax; for here the activity of Christ the priest, engaged in every action of the visible Church, becomes most intimately inserted into the liturgical act. Through the action of the celebrant there is placed on the altar the victim offered on Calvary and, at this moment, being offered by Christ through his ordained minister (and therefore sacramentally).

Because this victim is Christ's (because he, the *head,* offers it sacramentally) it is also the faithful's. Their worship, obedience and love—which are united through faith with Christ's—now find expression in the victim which simultaneously expresses Christ's worship, obedience and love. The interior union with Christ is expressed by a union of victim—by the identical victim. The mystery of justification in Christ, with all that this implies in terms of man's cooperation with God, here attains in the Church its highest and most actual form of earthly expression.

If this mystery of the Eucharistic sacrifice is to be more fully appreciated, particularly in its ethical implications, we must meditate on what it is that the faithful offer. It is the true body and blood of Christ, manifested in the Church in the form of the common food. The reflection of the Church, following the lead of St. Paul, the architect of the doctrine of the mystical body, has concentrated on the presence of the *body* of Christ in the Eucharist (cf. I Corinthians, 10:17). For Christ on Calvary, to offer this crucified body implied his entire submission, from within the sinfulness of mankind, to God.

When the body is contained in the Eucharist as the food (or source) of Christian life it takes on its wider significance. Now it connotes the greater body—the mystical body—of Christ, the community of those who are justified by Christ. When, therefore, the mystical body offers it in union with Christ at Mass, the implication of the action is that the mystical body offers itself to God, in imitation of Christ's self-offering on Calvary.

Certainly, at no other point in the life of the Church do Christians make a more explicit appeal to the intrinsic value of the victim of Calvary to cover over their own deficiencies. Yet at the same time, nowhere is the personal responsibility of Christians more deeply engaged. The appeal involves the responsibility; for the gift of God in grace calls for a personal response and commitment.

St. Augustine expresses this mystery of the Eucharistic and the mystical body in his lapidary way: in the sacrament of the altar, he says, "a sign is given to the Church that in the sacrifice she offers she herself is offered" (*City of God,* Bk. X, ch. 6).

The liturgical reform has no other purpose than to assist the baptized Christian, in the community of the Church and of mankind, to enter into this mystery of the Mass and of the Christian life. Consequently the practical details of the reform —however necessary and however much in harmony with the logic of the sacramental system and the nature of man— must be understood to have a purely relative value. They procure, if their full value is to be expressed, the integral humanization on the part of the faithful of the sacramental mystery of the incarnate Word.

The signs of Christ which form the liturgy are exploited fully only when consciously acknowledged and religiously adopted by the faithful assembled in community. Conversely, the religious participation of the community is not fully developed within the Church, the sacrament of the incarnate Word, unless the sign-structure of the liturgy is integrally adopted.

Yet the mystery of the Mass and of the Christian life remains. It is not exhausted by any form of ritual participation. It is exhausted only by the mystery of the Eucharist itself. The sacramental bread and wine are coextensive with the Church, because they contain Christ. Derivative symbolism and symbol-actions must be inadequate. Here, in the Eucharist itself, lies the possibility of another form of celebration without a congregation. But to say that there is no congregation is not to say that there is no community. Without the community the Eucharist would be meaningless.

II: PRIVATELY CELEBRATED MASS

THE PROBLEM

Eucharist and Church, the two are one mystery. This is why *Mysterium fidei* says: "The Church [. . .] as a whole offers the sacrifice of the Mass and in this is itself, as a whole, offered." This is why the Church must insist on "the public and social nature of any Mass whatsoever." [4] There is no such thing as a private Mass; the Mass is always an act of Christ and of the Church.

Much confusion could be avoided if there were general adoption of the prescriptions of the Instruction of the Sacred Congregation of Rites, *De musica sacra*: [5] "The holy sacrifice of the Mass is an act of public worship, presented to God in the name of Christ and the Church. The term 'private Mass,' accordingly, is to be avoided." The other term often used for Mass without a congregation—Mass "of devotion"—is equally confusing, betraying, as it does, a whole tradition of seminary training which emphasized an individualistic "piety."

---

4. Vatican II, Constitution, *Sacrosanctum Concilium*, on the Liturgy, ch. 1, n. 27, cited in *Mysterium fidei*, § 32; cf. Pius XII, Encyc., *Mediator Dei* (1947), § 101 (CTS, England, ed.): "... and this sacrifice, always and everywhere, necessarily and of its very nature, has a public and social character."

5. September 3, 1958; ch. 1, n. 2.

In perspectives such as these there is little hope of discovering an objectively valid reason for celebrating Mass if no congregation is present. The whole matter is simply reduced to one of religious feelings. Nor is this attitude essentially modified when, instead of speaking of the benefit an individual can draw from the Mass, the modern priest speaks of the "community."

The authentic meaning of the liturgical renewal can be discovered only when it is grasped that its fundamental inspiration lies in the reorientation of individual spirituality towards the historical mysteries of Christ in so far as these become existential events for the community of believers through the ministry of the word and the sacraments. In a very decided sense the renewal is "anti-demythologizing" for it points to the unique, once-for-all character of the saving event brought about in Jesus Christ, attributing this character precisely to the fact that this man *is* the divine Word incarnate. It is this divine saving event which must be made relevant to individual spirituality if the Christian life is to be marked with a liturgical character.

Inevitably, such a reorientation of spirit is going to prove most difficult for post-Reformation religious institutes and for the clergy and laity they have formed. For, on principle—a pastorally-inspired principle—these institutes eliminated the monastic liturgy from their way of life. The reasonableness of this is apparent since the monastic choir represents only one form of liturgical practice and is unsuitable for many forms of the apostolate. But the spirit of the liturgy, which forms an essential part of the Christian outlook, is difficult to preserve as a spirit—as a disembodied ideal—since this is just what it is not. And a great deal of the subjectivism brought into the Church through neglect of the liturgy has to be overcome before the renewal becomes natural and meaningful for the faithful. The reaction against Masses without a congregation is one manifestation of an indisputably honest attempt to cultivate a liturgical spirit, which has not yet, however, come to terms with the integral mystery of the liturgy.

In asserting that every Mass is an act of Christ and of the Church, the encyclical *Mysterium fidei,* goes on to state that in the sacrifice she offers the Church learns "to offer herself as a universal sacrifice and she applies the unique and infinite redemptive value of the sacrifice of the cross to the whole world for its salvation."[6] Two aspects of the Mass are distinguished in this phrase: those who offer it and those for whom it is offered. The problem of the privately-celebrated Mass is to determine how the *whole* Church offers and what benefit derives from such a Mass.

It is at this level that the practice has been subjected to recent theological discussion, for it is not immediately clear that the whole Church is involved. And this raises doubts as to the benefits to be derived from celebration without a congregation. In case the whole discussion should be swept aside as irrelevant, on the grounds that *Christ* offers the Mass, thus making the participation of the Church of no more than secondary importance, it is necessary to consider first the value of the Mass. This will bring to light the necessity of the participation of the faithful if the Mass is to have any meaning in the mystery of Christ and the Church. It will then be shown that, in fact, the whole Church participates in each Mass. This will permit, finally, the establishment of certain suggested practical conclusions regarding privately-celebrated Masses.

THE VALUE OF THE MASS

Assuming, for the moment, that the Church, or some well-defined part of it, is offering the Mass with Christ, the question

---

6. § 32 (*Acta Ap. Sed.,* loc. cit. [cf. note 1, above], 761).

asked is: what value has this Mass? Because Christ is the principal offerer, the Mass is said to have a value *ex opere operato.* As is well known, this is a phrase used of all the sacraments; it is a convenient—if often misunderstood—way of expressing the saving activity of Christ in the sacramental actions of the Church. It underlines the absolute gratuitousness of grace, in the giving of which the initiative can lie only with God.

But whereas, in its application to the other sacraments, this phrase refers to the gift of grace given through the sacrament to the ("disposed") recipient, when applied to the Mass it denotes the manifold pleading for grace which is characteristic of a sacrifice. It directs attention specifically to the active presence of Christ the priest in the Mass, which brings with it an infinite ennoblement of the Church's worship. On the part of Christ, it must always be stressed, this involves no redemptive value distinct from that of Calvary; it is simply that his unique sacrifice, never separable from its values, is re-presented sacramentally within the Church ceremony and is in this way made available to the Church.

The identity of the Mass with the sacrifice of Calvary, the fact that it is Christ who is the principal offerer, attributes an infinite value to all of the various aspects of the sacrifice. It is infinite as an act of worship, giving glory to God; infinite too as propitiation for sin and as a pleading for grace. But, once again, this worship, propitiation and impetration are not distinct from those of Calvary. What is different is that the unique sacrifice is being realized *in the liturgical act of the Church.*

This implies, first of all, that the whole purpose of this mystery is to permit the Church to unite her worship to that of Christ; and without this participation of the Church the sacramental renewal of the sacrifice would be pointless. To this we shall return.

A second implication of Christ's ecclesial offering concerns directly the *ex-opere-operato* efficacy of the Mass. The Church can *apply* the Mass, as Christ's sacrifice, to certain people. This is shown primarily from the fact that the Church does so. I am not certain whether it might not be argued that such application derives from the nature of the Mass as an ecclesial act of Christ, but it would seem that this is so. What is decisive for the direction to be taken by Catholic theology is that this has been the sacramental practice of the Church for many centuries. Cyril of Jerusalem indicates that the doctrine was already recognized in the fourth century. [7]

The application of an individual Mass in this sense is the prerogative of the celebrant, for it is he who is at once the minister of Christ, who is head of the body, and the official representative of the Church. The "intention" for which he offers the Mass, often in response to a stipend or a pastoral obligation, is precisely this application of the Mass as *Christ's* sacrifice (offered in and with the Church). Two things must be appreciated if our problem of the value of the Mass is to be clarified.

First, as the encyclical stresses, the application of the Mass for a particular intention does not have an exclusive character. "Every Mass which is celebrated is offered for the salvation, not just of a certain number of people, but of the whole world." [8] This is the basic intention of the Church, which is *not restricted* by the celebrant's special intention. What is clear, on the other hand, is that not every individual in the world (or in Purgatory) can have the Mass *specially* applied to him; otherwise, the word "special" would cease to be used meaningfully. Once again, it is the practice

---

7. *Catecheses,* 23 (= *Mystagogic,* 5), 8-18 (PG 33, 1115-1118); cited in *Mysterium fidei,* § 30 (*Acta Ap. Sed.,* loc cit. [cf. note 1, above], 760).

8. § 32 (*Acta Ap. Sed.,* loc. cit., 761).

which indicates that, within the universal intention, and without prejudice to it, a special intention may be included.

Secondly, it is most important to understand that the whole doctrine of the application of the Mass must be inserted into the context of the doctrine of grace—grace being understood in its widest sense. Specifically this means that there is nothing "magic" about the efficacy of the Mass. The sacrifice is without doubt a privileged moment in the union of the Church with Christ. His offering is made available to the Church as at no other time. Where the Mass is offered specially for an individual the common sacrifice of Christ and the Church becomes specially relevant for him as a pleading for grace and as an offer of grace. But he remains inviolably a responsible person whose personal confrontation with Christ and free acceptance of divine grace forms a necessary moment in the mystery of sanctification.

In this, the Mass does not differ from Calvary itself, which is the basic, universal pleading of mankind in Christ for grace, and its effective offer. The intention of the Church, formulated by the minister, does no more than apply or direct the sacrifice in favor of an individual and of all men.

The idea that has been introduced here, in the context of the problem of the application of the Mass, is that of the supremely personal character of the meeting between Christ and man which is effected in different ways in the Mass and in all the sacraments. It is now necessary to extend this principle of personalism from the area of the application of the Mass to that of the offering by the Church. It has already been stated that the whole purpose of Christ's sacrifice being realized in the liturgical act of the Church is that the Church may unite her worship to that of Christ. The personalist principle makes it clear that it is this present worship of the Church which determines effectively the value of the Mass.

The problem may be stated in this way. If it is admitted that Christ's offering of the Mass associates with the imperfect offering of the Church the infinite value of Calvary, then the obvious question arises: Why isn't a single Mass of infinite benefit to the Church and to mankind? I say it is an obvious question; it is one, however, which reveals that the questioner has not understood what is meant by the "sacramental renewal" of Christ's sacrifice.

One of the accepted theological solutions to this question is that the divine will has determined that each Mass shall have only a finite efficacy. It is quite open to anyone to accept this solution if it appears convincing to him; but it must be admitted that it relies on an over-simplified, and (I should think) theologically outmoded, concept of the manner in which God acts in the world. All the indications we have suggest that he does not intervene in human affairs in arbitrary fashion but rather that he respects utterly the deployment of human freedom. Further, as I have suggested, to take the question seriously, as this solution does, is to betray a misunderstanding of sacramental realities.

This leads to an alternative point of view: not to a solution of a pointless question, but to the personalist interpretation of the Mass.[9] This takes into account the Church-orientated character of the sacramental system (the fact, mentioned above, that the Mass belongs to the sphere of the risen Christ sending the Spirit on the Church) and the strictly personalist character of grace.

As an act of Church worship the effective value of the Mass depends on its being an insertion of the faithful's worship into Christ's. In the Mass the Church is brought before God as a priestly community of responsible persons, united in Christ the priest, offering his sacrifice. What is new in this phase of the mystery of salvation is the Church's present realization in terms of Christian worship of the redemptive worship

---

9. Cf. *Summa theologiae,* III, q. 79, a. 5.

of Christ on Calvary. It is this present realization, as united sacramentally to Christ's sacrifice (and therefore ennobled), which is the measure of the efficacy of a single Mass. This gives to the faithful a determinative rôle in the assessment of any Mass's effective value. The infinite value of Calvary is applied to the Church and the world in proportion to the devotion of the faithful expressed in the Church sacrifice. The use of mathematical terms must be excused; there appears to be no other way of speaking intelligibly of what is ultimately the mystery of grace and freedom.

If this interpretation of the value of the Mass is accepted, then it becomes imperative to determine to what degree the Church is involved in each Mass that is offered. When a congregation is present this may not present itself as a vital problem, for it may be assumed that, as a whole, the congregation is concerned to make the liturgical celebration an authentic act of community worship. The Mass, in this case, at once becomes meaningful as a present realization of the active sharing of (a section of) the Church in the mystery of Calvary. But what if there is no congregation? How are the faithful involved here? This is the crucial question for the problem of privately-celebrated Masses.

DOES THE WHOLE CHURCH OFFER?

The question of the involvement of the Church was raised in an influential article written by Fr. Karl Rahner, S.J., in the year 1949.[10] Considering the privately-celebrated Mass from the point of view of the spirituality of the individual priest, Fr. Rahner asked whether, in certain circumstances (practical impediments to devotion arising from the conditions in which such Masses must sometimes be celebrated) it might not be more profitable for the priest to renounce his own Mass in favor of taking part in a communal Mass.

The arguments which led him to pose this question were based on a personalistic interpretation of the Mass similar to that proposed above. A Mass is meaningful, he concluded, only when it implies an increase of devotion on the part of the offerers. As for the manner of offering, he continued, it is indifferent whether one be celebrant, member of the congregation or stipend-giver; in each case the spiritual profit drawn from the Mass will be determined by the devotion of the individual.

This point, which indubitably follows from the personalistic view of the Mass, was conceded by Pius XII in his address of November 2, 1954, though he was careful to compare devotional assistance at a communal Mass with thoughtless and negligent celebration.[11] The question in the Pope's mind did not touch on the fruit deriving from the Mass (for the celebrant), but regarded

> determining the nature of the act [involved in "hearing" or celebrating Mass] from which other fruits of the sacrifice flow, namely—apart from the divine worship of adoration and thanksgiving—the fruits of propitiation and impetration for those for whom the sacrifice is offered, even if they are not present at the sacrifice; also the fruits "for the sins,

---

10. "Die vielen Messen und das eine Opfer," *Zeitschrift für kath. Theol.*, 71 (1949), 257-317; reprinted separately, Freiburg i.B., 1951; revised, with additional material, by A. Häussling (*Quaestiones Disputatae,* n. 31), 1966. After the address of Pius XII to the bishops assembled for the celebration of the Queenship of Mary, November 2, 1954 (*Acta Ap. Sed.*, 46 [1954], 668-670), Fr. Rahner was invited to restate his argument. This restatement appeared as "Die vielen Messen als die vielen Opfer Christi," *Zeitschrift für kath. Theo.*, 77 (1955), 94-101.

11. It is hardly necessary to point out that Pius XII made no direct reference to Fr. Rahner's article. That Fr. Rahner felt that his position was placed in question is, however, clear from his second article, noted above.

penalties and satisfaction and other necessities of the living faithful as well as for those who have died in Christ and are not yet fully purged" (Trent, sess. 22, ch. 2).

Concluding, Pius XII affirmed that it is an error to equate one Mass at which a hundred priests assist devoutly with a hundred Masses celebrated by a hundred priests: "There are as many actions of Christ, the High Priest, as there are priests celebrating." [12]

In his second article Fr. Rahner rightly pointed out that, according to the teaching of Pius XII, the hundred priests forming a devout congregation would benefit more from their communal Mass than if each celebrated his own Mass in circumstances which prevented a similar degree of devotion. The point being made by the Pope, he continued, was the purely dogmatic one—that it is erroneous to identify one and many Masses from the point of view of the number of sacrificial actions of Christ. Moreover, it was worth while making this point since many authors are accustomed to speak of the Mass as "the making-visible of a sacrifice" (*Sichtbarwerdung eines Opfers*)—which is not the same as a "visible sacrifice" (*sichtbares Opfer*), the latter being the teaching of the Pope.

In brief—and this is Fr. Rahner's conclusion—it is not easy to draw conclusions from the papal statement for the question of the fruits of the Mass; though, clearly, the right answer depends in part from the fact that each Mass is a sacrificial act of Christ. Nothing more precise than this is to be found in Pius XII's statement.

Fr. Rahner's principle is that a disposition on the part of man is always determinative of the fruit of the Mass *ex opere operato*. This seems to me the only acceptable way of considering the Mass. [13] The important subsequent question, however, is: Where, concretely, are these dispositions to be found? It is here, I think, that Fr. Rahner cannot be followed for he states that only those faithful directly linked with a particular Mass may be considered to offer it and consequently to determine its fruits. Among these offerers he numbers exclusively the celebrant, the congregation and the stipend-giver. *Mysterium fidei,* on the contrary, affirms that the *whole* Church offers the Mass; and this is an essential point if privately-celebrated Masses are to be justified on grounds other than the spirituality of the individual priest.

On the face of it, it does not seem likely that Pius XII was concerned to enunciate an abstract dogmatic principle which had nothing, or very little, to do with the strictly practical problem he was confronting. His appeal to the offering of Christ in each Mass cannot be dismissed as contributing "in part" to solving the question of the fruits of each Mass; this was evidently a decisive element for the Pope, justifying the practice of Mass without a congregation.

At the same time, if the personalistic approach to the Mass is not to be abandoned, this offering by Christ in every Mass must be seen to be relevant to the faith and devotion present in the hearts of all the faithful of the Church. The presence of Christ, offering through the celebrant, must be considered as involving the whole Church in each offering of the Mass. If this can be shown to be the case, then it will be possible to concede that the celebrant, in certain circumstances, may draw less profit personally from his Mass than if he attended a communal Mass—and, at the same time, affirm that the Church as a whole and mankind draw greater benefit if he celebrates personally.

As what has already been said about liturgical spirit will perhaps indicate, Fr. Rahner's starting-point, the spirituality of the individual priest, tends to prejudice the whole question

---

12. Cf. also Pius XII, Address to the International Congress of Pastoral Liturgy, September 22, 1956.

13. Cf. Vatican II, Constitution, *Sacrosanctum Concilium,* on the Liturgy, ch. 1, n. 11.

from the outset. This is assuredly a personalistic point of view; and this can only be applauded. Unfortunately, the type of personalism involved is too narrowly subjectivistic, all true sense of the community in Christ, and, specifically, in Christ's historical act of redemption, being lost. This is a typical blind-spot in attempts made by theologians to apply existentialist philosophies to the Christian message. Bultmann's ingenious effort in this direction provides the most outstanding example.

Fr. Rahner resolutely rejects the involvement of the whole Church in the offering of individual Masses. In his opinion, to say that others, apart from those directly concerned with an individual Mass, can contribute to its ecclesial moral value "cannot be proved and is pious (or rather un-pious) fantasy." [14] He admits that the holiness at any one moment present in the whole Church is "manifested" in the Mass; but he argues that this gives the individual sacrifice, in so far as it is *distinct* from the others, no value that is distinct from that of the others. For they all, by hypothesis, are carried by the same unchanging habitual devotion of the Church. Therefore, the single worth, which takes hold of several sacrifices, has the same single efficacy on the whole Church, whether the number of cult-manifestations is greater or less. [15]

I think it is fair to contrast Fr. Rahner's "pious fantasy" with what *Mysterium fidei* says of the offering by the whole Church: "this truly wonderful teaching." First, however, let it be said that the sacramental character of the Mass clearly postulates, for its integral implementation, a particular congregation and, further, a congregation participating in the fashion required by the Constitution on the Liturgy. It is in this sense that the encyclical states:

> . . . from this it follows that, while the integral, active participation (*actuosa participatio*) of the faithful is very much in harmony with the celebration of the Mass, and this almost from the very nature of the act . . . etc. [16]

It is the logical consequence of the presence of Christ's sacrifice under *symbols* that the congregation should take the most active part possible in the ceremonial. This is the basis of the liturgical reform, as understood by the Council in the light of the general circumstances of the Church in the second half of this century and its implications must be exploited loyally to the fullest degree possible. But the mystery is more than this, more than anything that can be expressed symbolically; and if this is ignored the liturgical reform is unavoidably doomed to failure.

Granted, then, that the logical consequence of a sacramental sacrifice of the Church is fully implemented only in an integrally active congregation, the inner side of the mystery has not yet been fully penetrated. For to stay at the level of social symbolism, which is common to the Church and to any other human society, is to ignore the distinctive character of the ecclesial community as the sacrament of divine salvation in the world. There are two texts of the teaching authority which may be consulted on this: Pius XII's *Mediator Dei* and Vatican II, Dogmatic Constitution, *Lumen Gentium,* on the Church, ch. 2, n. 11; the former provides an extended commentary which may be usefully applied to the conciliar text.

The whole second part of *Mediator Dei,* concerned with the Eucharistic sacrifice, retains its value today, providing a doctrinal background to the Council's Constitution on the Liturgy, even though certain of the practical problems it faces

---

14. "Die vielen Messen und das eine Opfer," *Z.k.Th.*, loc. cit. [note 10, above], 276; 1966 ed., 53.

15. *Z.k.Th.*, loc. cit., 277; 1966 ed., 55; the above text is an almost verbatim translation.

16 § 32 (*Acta Ap. Sed.*, loc cit. [cf. note 1, above], 761; cf. Vatican II, *Sacrosanctum Concilium,* on the Liturgy, ch. 1, n. 27. See Colman O'Neill, "The meaning of *participatio actuosa,*" Paper read to the Fifth International Congress of Sacred Music, Chicago and Milwaukee, August, 1966 (to appear in *Sacred Music*).

may no longer be relevant. In defense of privately-celebrated Masses there appears the following:

> Every time the priest re-enacts what the divine Redeemer did at the Last Supper, the sacrifice is really accomplished; and this sacrifice, always and everywhere, necessarily and of its very nature, has a public and social character. For he who offers it acts in the name both of Christ and of the faithful, of whom the divine Redeemer is the head, and he offers it to God for the Holy Catholic Church, and for the living and the dead. [17]

As this passage makes clear, the mystery of the participation of the whole Church in each Mass is tied in some fashion to the representative character of the celebrant. Now it is important to underline the fact that the baptized who participate directly in a Mass (congregation, stipend-giver) are *not* reliant solely on the priest's representing them in the sacrifice. The opinion that they are used to be proposed by several theologians, but hardly appears to do justice to the status of the baptized as sharers, sacramentally, in the priesthood of Christ.

Pius XII made an important distinction relevant here, between offering "through" the celebrant and offering "with" him.[18] Going slightly beyond the letter of *Mediator Dei,* it appears legitimate to propose that direct participants in the Mass offer *with* the celebrant in so far as each one of them, in virtue of his baptismal character, [19] can immediately adopt the Eucharistic (ecclesial) victim as the sacrificial sign of his own devout participation in the "sentiments" of Christ. [20] The baptized members of the congregation are evidently dependent on the priest for the making-present of Christ's sacrifice. When it is placed on the altar, they personally may offer it, as members of Christ the priest.

In view of the demands of the symbolism on which the Mass is based—where a certain physical proximity is required if one is to be meaningfully associated with the ceremony—it seems reasonable to confine offering *with* the celebrant to those who directly participate in this way in a particular sacrifice. The possibility of offering *through* the priest still remains, for the other members of the Church. What is the meaning of such an offering?

In what fashion—to reformulate the question—may the celebrant be said to represent the whole Church and to associate the whole Church with the sacrifice which he is offering? Some theologians, and Fr. Rahner appears to be among them, [21] would see the priest as representing the Church juridically, that is, through a commission received from the Church; and it is not surprising that such representation is then said to have no moral value that can, in any personal sense, be associated with the Mass.

Pius XII, on the contrary, proposes a more real, and more mysterious, link between the celebrant and all the members of the Church:

> . . . the priest acts in the name of the people precisely and only because he represents the person of our Lord Jesus Christ, considered as head of all the members and offering himself for them. [22]

The same thought is repeated when the faithful are said to offer *through* the priest:

> That the faithful offer the sacrifice through the priest is

---

17. Pius XII, Encyc., *Mediator Dei* (CTS, England, ed.) § 101.
18. Ibid., § § 96-98.
19. Ibid., § 92.
20. Ibid., § 98.
21. Art. cit., 275.
22. *Mediator Dei,* § 88.

> clear from the fact that the minister of the altar acts in the person of Christ considered as head, and as offering in the name of all the members; and this is why it is true to say that *the whole Church* makes the offering of the victim through Christ. [23]

It seems to be clear from this that, even though the demands of strict sacramentality (direct participation) cannot be met by the whole Church in relation to a particular Mass, all the faithful do participate in each Mass because the principal offerer is Christ, acting through his minister.

It should be noted that in *Mediator Dei* stress is laid on Christ's headship; and this indicates in which direction we should look for an explanation of the association of the whole Church.

The victim of every Mass signifies, or expresses, or "incarnates sacramentally," in sacrificial form the capital worship of Christ—that is, the worship which is the source and reference-point of all the present holiness of the members of Christ. [24] It follows, in virtue of the vital union between head and members, that the sacramentalization of Christ's worship in the Mass carries with it, or implies, also the sacramentalization, in the same ceremony, of all the holiness which, here and now in the Church, derives from, and makes actual in the members, the fundamental worship of Christ. This means that there is a *new* moral value in the Mass, distinct from Christ's, but wholly derived from his. This is the central point of the view which I propose. If Christ's fontal worship is related to a particular Mass, then so is all the holiness found in the Church. If the one in whom all the believers are incorporated offers the Mass, then so do all the believers.

There is a difference between the faithful directly participating in a Mass and the rest of the Church. The former are associated with the sacrifice both spiritually and immediately-corporeally (through a direct, fully human proximity to, and use of, the Eucharistic symbols). The latter are associated primarily through their spiritual union with Christ, while their corporeal relationship is minimal. In the first case the pneumo-corporeal nature of the Church is fully realized in the congregation gathered at the altar. In the second case it is the union of the Church through the Spirit which is decisive; the visible dimension of the Church is less perfectly realized.

Indeed, when Mass is celebrated without a congregation, nothing remains, at the level of symbol, but the priest himself (and the server). It must be added that, however deficient such a visible manifestation of the assembly of believers may be, it still remains that there *is* a manifestation of the community. This is precisely because the priest acts, not primarily as an individual, but as a sacramental representative of Christ, the *head* of the Church—and for this reason even the server may be dispensed with in some cases. The celebrant is not simply satisfying his personal piety; he holds an office, the specific purpose of which is to represent Christ, the head, in the Church; and this implies representation of those who depend on the head. If a visible, ecclesial relationship to the celebrant is sought on the side of the faithful, this may be found in the fact (and ecclesial implications) of baptism. In establishing the individual as an integral element in the Church, the sacrament of Christ, baptism also establishes a visible bond between all the members of the Church, and between the members and the official acts of the Church.

In this explanation I have avoided appealing to the liturgical, or sacramental, function of the baptismal character as a means

---

23. Ibid., § 97; italics added.

24. I have said, "The victim . . . signifies" in order to abstract from the theological controversy whether Christ actually offers each Mass, or the Church, through the priest, simply acts in his name. On the hypothesis that he actually offers, the association of all his members will be even more clearly indicated.

by which the faithful, not present at a Mass, might associate themselves with it. On the contrary, it is precisely through the character that those present are capable of adopting the Eucharistic victim as the sacrificial expression of their own union with the self-offering of Christ, and so of offering this victim. For the present problem I have appealed instead to union with Christ by grace and to the general visible structure of the Church. This distinction has been made, not for any reason arising from the theology of the Church, but because of the difficulty, noted by Fr. Rahner, of establishing the feasibility of an efficacious intention on the part of an individual with respect to every Mass celebrated. This is a problem of psychology, not directly of ecclesiology; and I am not prepared to dispute the matter. That some people form an intention of the kind rejected by Fr. Rahner is undoubted; many prayer-books contain appropriate formulas. The question concerns its efficacy. It is certainly not robbed of usefulness in the explanation I have given, since union with Christ by grace does all that such an intention purposes. With the problem thus situated on an ontological basis—the objective structure of the Church—the forming of an intention might well be encouraged for psychological reasons. At least it serves to remind the faithful of their constant union with the Mass.

A further difficulty remains. Is it meaningless that the *same* holiness and devotion, that existing at any given time in the Church, should be presented to God in several Masses celebrated simultaneously?

It is hard to avoid the impression that this new difficulty raised by Fr. Rahner is a little abstract. The assumption that it is question of the same devotion would have to be looked into more carefully. There is, in the first place, the important difference introduced into an individual Mass by the celebrant's special intention which permits the special participation of an individual or a group—usually the stipend-giver. (The theological importance of the stipend may be noted in passing.

If, for one reason or another, the system of stipends should be renounced, generally or locally, the special association which it permits with the Mass should, in some form, be retained.) Then, too, the presence of a congregation introduces a new element at least at the level of sacramentality or symbol.

Even abstracting from the uniqueness of each Mass, deriving from one or other or both of the elements just mentioned, it would still appear evident that each Mass is meaningful, and this for two reasons: because Christ offers and because the Church offers.

Christ offers. In each Mass the saving power of Calvary is applied (through the cooperation of the Church) to the living and the dead. The personalist principle remains untouched; sheer multiplication of Masses is not going to procure salvation for any individual without his personal cooperation. But repeated and incessant recourse to the sacrifice of Christ is the foundation on which the Church rests; and it takes its highest liturgical form in the Mass.

It is just this which makes the repeated offering meaningful on the part of the Church; for a new dimension is introduced into her offering precisely because her concern to procure repeated celebration of the Mass bears witness to her belief in the saving power of Christ. It is the mathematical approach which here is meaningless, with its assumption that the union of the Church with Christ in charity is, as it were, exhausted by concentration on a single Mass. The many Masses daily celebrated, with or without a congregation, are a confession of the Church's incapacity to worship as she ought, and of her belief that she can find strength only in Christ.

The privately-celebrated Mass should certainly be a Mass "of devotion" in the sense that it is a personal Christian action on the part of the celebrant. But its significance in the life of the Church rests, not on such subjective grounds, but on our belief that it is the action of Christ the head and, through him, of all his members in the Church.

PRACTICAL CONCLUSIONS

It may appear that a purely mechanical repetition of Masses would be the practical result of what is here being advocated. This is not so. Implicit in the concept of the need of the Church for many Masses is the recognition that the Mass serves a *human* need to worship God and beg his blessings through Christ. Like any human activity, use of the Mass must not be irrational. On the contrary, celebration of Mass must be integrated into the life of the Church and used in accordance with the reasonable norms which govern a society which is at once divine and human.

The tension between the two elements of the Church becomes apparent as soon as an attempt is made to formulate a practical rule for frequency of the Mass. This cannot be determined solely in terms of what would appear reasonable in a purely human society. But neither is it legitimate, by appealing to the divine initiative in the Mass, to call for the most frequent celebration possible, irrespective of human psychological factors.

The complexity of the situation is well reflected in the decision of the encyclical, *Mysterium fidei*:

> . . . while the active ceremonial participation of the faithful is very much in harmony with the celebration of the Mass, and this almost from the very nature of the act, at the same time no fault is to be found with a Mass which is celebrated by a priest privately, according to the norms and legitimate traditions of Holy Church and for a just cause, even if there is only a server assisting and making the responses; indeed, such Mass is to be approved. [25]

Clearly, full appreciation is accorded here to the communal symbolism of the Mass; at the same time the mystery is not ignored, though the conditions laid down for privately-celebrated Mass require that the practice be subject to prudent judgment.

Indeed, this decision is so concerned to present every aspect of the practical problem that it might be considered not to give a solution at all were it not for the concluding paragraph of this section of the encyclical. Here the specific recommendation is made that priests "celebrate Mass worthily every day, so that they themselves and the rest of the Christian faithful may share in the application of the fruits of the sacrifice of the cross which flow from it in such abundance." [26]

In this unequivocal statement the narrow individualism of a certain type of priestly spirituality is magnificently overcome and recognition of the true sense of the priest's mediatorial function in the Church leads to a practical rule of life. It is curious and a little saddening that the individualism and subjectivism thus rejected, which are so opposed to the authentic sense of the liturgy, should be reviving among those who sincerely believe themselves to be the foremost proponents of the liturgical spirit.

Particular circumstances are not, evidently, taken into consideration in such a general rule. The individual priest must make his own decision, but he is under an obligation to attempt to bring to his personal decision a similar balance to that found in the papal letter.

A pastoral theology of the priesthood must, therefore, grant to privately-celebrated Mass the same place that is given it in the encyclical. Among the reasonable circumstances which justify this form of celebration must certainly be numbered personal preference for it, when pastoral obligations do not require celebration with the people. When the individual's position and temperament are taken into account in this fashion,

---

25. § 32 (*Acta Ap. Sed.*, loc cit. [cf. note 1, above], 761).
26. § 33 (ibid., 762).

it still remains that concelebration, where possible, is objectively a more adequate solution.[27] Here the community, always present in the reality, is manifested at the level of symbol; the sacrament is humanly more perfect. With the reintroduction of concelebration, a new, sacramental emphasis has been laid on the collegiality of the priesthood and on its relation to the episcopacy. The value of this cannot be overemphasized.

Just as much as for privately-celebrated Mass, temperamental preference for concelebration is legitimate and praiseworthy. There would be cause for concern only if such preference concealed a misapprehension of the nature of the Mass itself. For this reason there are good pastoral reasons why a priest who experiences a temperamental disinclination to celebrate without a congregation or without concelebrators should accept, when necessary, and perhaps even on other occasions, the discipline of offering Mass privately. The difficulty which he may encounter in doing this, if approached in a spirit of faith, should lead to an interiorization of the mystery of the Mass and to a more profound understanding of the mystery of the Church. This in turn is calculated to lead to a deeper appreciation of the meaning behind the Council's concern for integral active participation of the faithful.

To understand the significance of privately-celebrated Mass is to go beyond the immediate appearances and to enter into the mystery of faith itself. This is where symbolism is transcended. And to understand more profoundly the mystery of the Eucharist is to experience more deeply the mystery of the community which is formed and built up by this sacrament. Like the Eucharist, the Church is a mystery which cannot be grasped by the senses; it is a mystery open only to faith, and to a faith which is prepared to seek for Christ in a sacramental structure which at once reveals and conceals him.

Paul VI has drawn attention to further perspectives illumined by the significance attached to privately-celebrated Mass.[28] While discussing the relation between religious profession and the priesthood, he noted that, as is evident, the former neither implies nor demands the latter.[29] Nevertheless, the Church has, in the course of her historical evolution, discovered a profound link between the two. In her practice she has indicated that there is a harmony in the union in one person of religious consecration and the priestly character, for this implies a special conformity to Christ who was at once priest and victim.

Consequently, though modern monasticism has rediscovered the meaning of religious profession without the priesthood, and though the practical consequences of this rediscovery have been approved by the Council,[30] this does not imply that there is, or has been, any confusion of vocations in ordaining monks. And, further, the criterion for ordination is not the pastoral needs either of the monastery or of the other faithful. If the Decree, *Presbyterorum ordinis,* in describing the integral personality of the priest, pointed to his divinely-given powers and also to their exercise in the care of the People of God, this did not in any sense imply that it was the mind of the Council that there is no point in ordaining monks whose ministry will, for all practical purposes, be confined to the celebration of Mass. For the same Decree goes on to declare that the offering of the Sacrifice is the principal activity of the priest.[31]

---

27. Cf. Vatican II, Decree, *Presbyterorum ordinis,* on the ministry and life of priests, ch. 2, n. 7; Sacred Cong. Rites, Instruction, *Inter Oecumenici,* September 26, 1964, n. 15.

28. Address to 6th Meeting of the Conference of Italian Major Religious Superiors (CISM), November 18, 1966 (cf. *Osservatore Romano,* November 19, 1966, p. 1).

29. Cf. Vatican II, Decree, *Perfectae caritatis,* on the apt renewal of religious life, n. 10; Dogm. Constitution, *Lumen Gentium,* on the Church, ch. 6, n. 43.

30. Cf. Decree, *Perfectae caritatis,* n. 15.

31. *Presbyterorum ordinis,* ch. 3, n. 13.

The ordained priest cannot base his spirituality on that of the layman. He shares, obviously, in the common priesthood of the baptized, but he has too a mediatorial role to play within the community of the Church, something which sets him apart, while not in any sense separating him, from the laity. If he consistently attempts to abstract from this situation which is his, he is needlessly introducing a division into his life.

His whole Christian outlook, while recognizing his community with all those saved by Christ, should be orientated by his consecration to speak in the name of Christ, the head of the body. This is the life he must lead, even as a member of Christ. And his office, which determines the concrete form of his membership, reaches its fullest expression in the celebration of the Eucharistic sacrifice. This is his primary ministry in the Church and it should mould his Christian personality.

4

THE PRESENCE OF CHRIST

REAL PRESENCE AND SACRIFICE

The point has already been made that the sacrificial character of the Mass forbids any explanation of the Eucharist in which Christ's presence is conceived in purely dynamic fashion. The victim offered by Christ and by the Church is that true body of Christ which is the prototype and source of the mystical body. If the sacrifice of the Mass draws together in an offering to the Father all the activity of the Church this is only because the event of Calvary, where Christ suffered and died, is sacramentally represented on the altar.

There is, in other words, an intimate connection of interdependence between sacrifice and real presence. This is already indicated in I Corinthians, in the tenth chapter. These are two aspects of the sacrament; they belong to the same mystery and one may not be separated from the other. Christ is immolated sacramentally at the moment when he begins to be sacramentally present as spiritual food under the appearances of bread and wine.

Something very specific is here being said about the manner in which Christ's presence is effected. The simple supper theme, which assuredly provides the setting for the mystery, remains inadequate to express the fulness of the mystery. Christ's presence as food for his members—which could, conceivably, come about in more than one way—is, in fact, determined by its sacrificial function. No Catholic theologian would deny this explicitly. But the significance of the point will appear more clearly later when it will be seen that certain modern theologians are tempted to eliminate the new element introduced into the mystery of the Eucharist by its sacrificial character. For them, the sacrifice is to be found precisely in the offering of the sacrament to men as their spiritual food—communion is sacrifice. The validity of this claim, so typical of contemporary concern for man's social dimension, will be discussed later. Here it is sufficient to note that unilateral insistence on the dynamic aspect of the Eucharist leads inevitably to a modification in the concept of sacrifice. Sacrifice becomes something no longer offered to God but to men.

This is not without relevance to liturgical practice. In harmony with the Gospel accounts of the institution of the sacrament, current writing on the Eucharist stresses that the Mass is a meal, the Lord's Supper. This approach is inspired by both pastoral and ecumenical motives. In saying: "Take and eat," Christ was inviting Christians to share in that food which is himself so that they might be united in charity with God and with one another. It is through this charity that the eschatological symbolism of the common banquet is already realized in incipient fashion in the earthly Church (cf. Luke, 22: 16; I Corinthians, 11: 26).

The ethical consequences of this common meal for the Christian community are evident. Through this sharing in the one bread the mystery of salvation, achieved once for all by Christ, becomes effective for the Church and imposes on the members the task of living the united life of charity. Here, in general terms at least, Catholic teaching unites with that of the other Christian Churches.

For the pastoral reasons indicated, isolated experimental attempts have been made to underline the meal-character of the Mass by having a small congregation sit round a table at which the Mass is celebrated. This example serves well to illustrate how one aspect of a complex, mysterious reality can be emphasized at the expense of other aspects. While the Mass is a meal of friendship, it is also a sacrifice.

The Last Supper undoubtedly establishes for the Mass a unique *form* of sacrifice, and one which projects into the Mass all the overtones of the biblical symbolism of the paschal meal. But, like the paschal meal itself, with its reference to the Exodus, it is a re-actualizing memorial of a divine saving event. It surpasses the Jewish meal in that it not merely makes the Alliance between God and his Chosen People actual and relevant for those gathered at the table—it *is* the sacrifice which sealed the New Alliance, made present in a mysterious way which takes away nothing from the uniqueness of the event of Calvary.

The idea of the Mass-supper at which the redemptive act of Christ is applied through Communion is, in these perspectives, inadequate. Those who gather for Mass are not simply a congregation of the priestly people of Christ. There is among them one who is empowered by ordination to speak in the name of Christ and make present for the priestly people the unique sacrifice under the symbol of food. Because the saving act of Christ, head of the body, is brought into the liturgical act of the Church in this fashion, through a human minister, a radically new element has to be reckoned with in the Mass, something which the concept of "meal" fails to encompass.

It may, then, be legitimate to raise the doubt whether the religious attitude proper to co-offerers of the sacrifice is encouraged by sitting round a table waiting to eat. If understanding and adaptation of the symbolism of the Mass are necessary for full participation, at least it must be insisted that the symbols employed should be not totally inadequate to the reality which is being enacted. To attempt to reconstruct today the situation in the supper-room is a form of escapism from the reality of history.

Yet, if there is undoubtedly something special about the presence of Christ in the Eucharist, it is one of the merits of modern theology to have refused to consider the Eucharistic presence in isolation from the integral mystery of Christ's presence in his Church. It is from within the mystical presence of Christ in the world (through faith, sealed by baptism) that the Eucharistic presence is realized; and it is realized only in function of the mystical presence.

In these perspecitves which are those of St. Augustine and his tradition as much as of modern theologians, it is the *purpose* of the Eucharist within the economy of salvation which is stressed. Christ comes, not to be enthroned in the host, but to live in our heart—so Fr. Schoonenberg, whose work will be considered below, puts it.

The value of thus situating the Eucharist in terms of the ultimate objective of the Church is clear. A sense of the purpose of the sacrament already excludes many forms of false and superstitious devotion to the so-called "prisoner of the tabernacle." Nevertheless, if priority is in this way justly attributed to union with God in Christ, a further point is to be considered when the Eucharist is viewed as one among many means in which Christ is present in the Church.

Here the Eucharist enjoys its own priority. Since it is question now of the order of means, directed towards achieving men's union with God, this can evidently be no more than a relative priority; yet it must be preserved. Christ is present in many ways in the Church; he is present in the Eucharist in a pre-eminent way.

THE DIFFICULTY OF LANGUAGE

Christians are clearly faced with an almost insurmountable obstacle when they attempt to find language to express the pre-eminent ecclesial presence of Christ in the Eucharist. Our language has considerable flexibility in the expression of human situations. I can speak, for example, of a person being "present" either because he is in the same room as myself or simply because he is in my thoughts. But the presence of Christ in the Eucharist escapes all normal human experience, so that when I affirm that he is "present" in the sacrament I am applying this word to a new situation, one not envisaged by current, everyday usage.

Evidently, within the society of the Church, this extension of usage is a matter of common consent, so that it is not a case of an individual arbitrarily constructing his own private system of linguistic symbols. Nevertheless, the society of the Church must take the responsibility of justifying, as well as it is able, the modifications it has introduced into the language of human society. Primarily, this is a responsibility to the individual members of the Church for they, as much as anyone else, must be made aware of the specialized sense attached by the Church to some of the words she uses.

The only feasible way in which the Church can meet this responsibility is by providing examples of her linguistic usage, thereby illustrating what elements of common human experience she appeals to in the expression of her revelation, and at the same time indicating in what way her experience of faith transcends all human experience. If the words she uses in the expression of the mysteries of salvation are entirely divorced from the human situations they normally signify, these words will be meaningless. At the same time, the words used by her must be shown to have acquired a new dimension of signification if they are to be understood as applying to the intervention of the God of salvation in history and in human experience.

It is not necessary—indeed it is not possible—that the Church should understand fully the new dimension of signification attached to her words; for this would mean that she understood the mysteries of God, and to this she lays no claim. It is sufficient if, appealing to revelation, she affirms the existence of this new dimension and if she draws attention to the modification which it imposes on the normal signification of language.

The statement, then, that Christ is present in the Eucharist may be rendered intelligible in the way that the Church understands it only if it is set in the context of other affirmations concerning the presence of Christ in the Church.

In this fashion, beginning from experience, it is possible to indicate a factor common to every presence of the risen Christ in the Church, while at the same time formulating what it is that is distinctive about the Eucharistic presence.

ECCLESIAL PRESENCE OF CHRIST

A saying of Chirst is presupposed by every affirmation concerning his presence in the Church: "Where two or three are gathered together for my sake, there am I in the midst of them" (Matthew, 18: 20). This promise is frequently quoted to show that Christ prays when the Church prays. But the significance of Christ's words is not to be restricted to prayer.

Those who are gathered in Christ's name are those who believe in him and in his saving mission; and it is always within such a community of faith that Christ is made present. For it would be to do violence to the nature of the Church to draw a sharp line of distinction between the presence of Christ among believers, those who hear his word and do it, and his presence in those who exercise the ministry of the word and in the sacraments. We have to search deeper, beyond the too-neat distinction between community of faith and institution of salvation, if we are to discover the unity of the mystery of the Church.

The presence of Christ in the Church assumes many forms; but basic to all of them is the community of faith. This is the place where the word of salvation is heard; from within it, and to promote it, Christ takes on new modes of presence. He is always the transcendent Savior, drawing together the community of believers. Faith is his first gift; when he gives himself in other ways it is always in favor of faith and the life which expresses it.

If Christ is present when the Church prays and when the Church performs acts of mercy it is because he dwells by faith in our hearts and sends the Spirit of charity to us. This is the presence of a person who is known and loved and who inspires our activity. When we say that Christ is present in this way, we are simply formulating the familiar doctrine of sanctifying grace in specifically Christian terms.

A new factor enters when the Church preaches the Gospel. As the word of God this is preached only in his name and by the authority of Christ, the Word incarnate, and with his assistance. Here the emphasis has moved from the presence of Christ in his members and in their activities to his presence as head of the Church, as Savior, active through the successors of the apostles and through their cooperators.

Christ is here present as speaking if his ministers remain faithful to the Gospel. Yet, whatever special guarantee of authenticity is in this way attached to the preaching of the Gospel—in other words, whatever special presence of Christ is assured in the ministry of the word—this occurs within the sphere of the presence of Christ by faith in the hearts of men. For the ministry of the word is conceivable only within the community of faith or as an activity of the community of faith in its mission to the world.

It is not simply that faith is needed to hear the word of God preached by the Church. Rather the existence of the community of faith is presupposed to the authoritative preaching of the Gospel; the presence of Christ as infallible teacher brings a new density of truth to the community of those who live by the revealed truth of salvation. The Spirit of truth is active in a human society so that subjective belief is guaranteed and developed by an objective norm and is constantly called to a new encounter with the unique Word of God incarnate. It is the historical reality, and once-for-all character of the revelation in Christ, upon which the community of faith depends, which requires this guiding presence of Christ within the Church. The ministry of the word could not be left as a mere human attempt to announce the saving event. That would be to empty the Incarnation of its unique significance.

In a closely similar fashion Christ's presence in the Church through those who exercise the pastoral office (which is broader than the ministry of the word, though allied to it) takes shape within the community of faith, in whose favor this office is exercised. As with the preaching of the Gospel, so here it is the social situation of the believer, within the mystery of the Incarnation, which accounts for the structure of the Church. Christ's presence in men's hearts by faith can attain its full dimensions only when it develops through the structures of human society: through the teaching and the direction received from other men. Yet society has no ultimate claim on men's minds and can make no ultimate appeal to their wills unless there is a society which is so united to the Word incarnate that it can make Christ present here and now. The historical tradition, claiming continuity with those who heard Christ speak, makes too extravagant a claim unless the risen Christ is with it and speaks through it.

In the Mass and the sacraments an even more immediate presence of Christ the head within the community is realized. The condition of his presence in the pastoral activity of the hierarchy is that the members of the hierarchy, through all the ambiguity of concrete action, remain faithful to his word. It is their activity which is to the foreground, guaranteed indeed by Christ, yet subject to all the influences of their personal, social and historical situation. In the sacraments it is more clearly and more directly Christ himself who intervenes in the life of the community of believers, coming to meet the community in a way somehow like, yet somehow different from, the way he met the apostles and disciples.

To ensure contact with Christ the Savior himself—or rather because Christ himself assumes responsibility for the encounter—the personality of the minister recedes into the background. *Mysterium fidei* quotes St. John Chrysostom: "The offering is the same, no matter who offers it, whether it be Peter or Paul; it is the same as that which Christ gave to his disciples and which priests now perform; today's offering is in no way inferior to the earlier one, for it is not men who sanctify it, but the same Christ who sanctified the other." [1] It is the same mystery of Christ himself, active in the sanctification of believers, and worshipping with the Church, which is discovered in all the sacraments.

In virtue of these sacramental actions Christ is present in a more sublime way, but also in a more human way; and it is the latter which explains best the mystery, since this sets the sacraments in the perspectives of the fundamental mystery of the Incarnation. As always, this new ecclesial presence of Christ is a presence realized within the community of believers; and it is a presence which has no saving significance unless it is greeted with faith.

Yet, precisely because it is a presence which faith discovers in the ceremonial, and therefore corporeal, actions of the Christian community, it complements the presence of Christ by faith in men's hearts. This is also true, in some degree, of Christ's presence in the teaching and pastoral word of the

---

1. *In ep. 2 ad Tim.*, homil. 2, 4 (PG 62, 612); *Mysterium fidei*, § 38 (*Acta Ap. Sed.*, 57 [1965], 763).

Church's ministers. But through word alone an integrally human contact with Christ is not established. Man meets man through the medium of the whole body, not through word of mouth alone. It is just this fully human contact which is established with Christ through the sacraments. And still—that last statement cannot stand without qualification. For it is too evident that the contact through the sacraments is not integrally human. It is not the body of Christ that we see; not yet. Say rather, the sacraments tend, in a unique way, towards an integral human contact with Christ.

The strain which the Church is placing on human language is now becoming clear. When another man can communicate with me not only by word, written or spoken, but also by facial expression, by gesture, above all by touch, then clearly he is present to me in the fullest sense of the word. When the Church makes a similar assertion about Christ in the sacraments the situation is evidently of another kind.

If he is present, his presence is a mediated one; it is the corporeal actions of other men which lend to his presence by faith its more integrally human dimensions. Until the Second Coming his faith-presence achieves corporeal dimension through symbolic actions of the Church in which he is active. Assuredly, the risen Christ exists now in integral human form—but "elsewhere"; and he is not encountered in this form by us who live in the earthly Church.

The practical impossibility of expressing in existential language such a form of presence is apparent. Our words apply properly only to the human situations of our experience. To attempt to modify them by saying that Christ's presence is "spiritual" is clearly inadequate; for this is to abandon the whole concept of sacramentalism, permitting no distinction from his presence by faith. Yet to speak of "bodily" presence is only a little more satisfactory and opens the way for all sorts of crude misinterpretations, for in normal usage "bodily" presence signifies immediate local presence; and this is not realized in the sacraments.

The corporeal element of our contact with Christ is achieved through symbolic actions which may, perhaps, as has been suggested, be thought of as tending towards immediate local presence, but can never be simply categorized as achieving such presence. The term "symbolic" presence provides no solution for this describes the sacramental action only in so far as it depends on the community of believers; however, this fails to take account of Christ's personal intervention, in his bodiliness. There seems to be no alternative but to speak of a "sacramental" presence of Christ, thereby acknowledging its uniqueness, and to attempt, as has been attempted here, to add the explanations necessary to clarify this term.

All of this is the mystery of the Church: Christ's presence in the world, "lovely in limbs not his." Once this mystery, with its varied facets, is accepted, it is hardly surprising to find that at the heart of the Church there is a presence of Christ which brings him in his integral humanity among believers, though still veiled from our eyes. This is his Eucharistic presence fulfilling the logic of his presence in the Church.

As wtih the other forms of the presence of Christ the head, this presence can come about only within the community of believers and for the sake of the community, lending a more perfect corporeal (sacramental) dimension to the meeting of man and Christ in faith. It perfects the social dimension of the community of salvation, for here Christ is present, not only as speaking and guiding his members through the pastors of the Church, not only as offering through the celebrant of the Mass, not only as acting through the ministers of the sacraments, but in the fullest manner possible in the Church on earth.

To think of this presence apart from its significance for the indwelling of Christ in the hearts of believers is to falsify it utterly. Yet, though it cannot be realized outside the community of believers, it does not depend exclusively on the faith of the community. [2] If this were all that it were, its precise function of humanizing faith (by lending the presence of Christ a corporeal dimension) would be defeated.

The presence of Christ the head in the pastors and sacraments of the Church (as distinct from, and complementary to, his presence in his members through faith and charity) is a new and further gratuitous gift of God, assisting faith, giving body to the person in whom we believe. This is the condescension of God made man. We are no longer addressed by the naked demand of the word; we can discover the Word made flesh in our fellow-man. This is the mystery of Incarnation, where God is in the world saving men through the humanity of Christ, made present in the structures of the Church.

SUBSTANTIAL PRESENCE

Dare it be said now that it is quite easy to see why the Church speaks of the Eucharistic presence as *substantial*? There is no need, yet, for horrified cries that phenomenology has been betrayed with the introduction of alien categories. The word "substantial" is used here in its pre-philosophical sense, signifying that Christ's presence in the Eucharist is "whole and entire," that is, not merely dynamic as in the other sacraments. It is the common-sense notion of presence that is here employed, corresponding to the notion we have when we say of a person that he is "here." Yet, at once, the necessary modification must be added. For in the Eucharist, as our senses plainly testify, Christ is clearly not "here" in the physical, material (as well as personal) fashion in which another person is in the room with me. The Eucharistic presence, we have agreed to say, is "sacramental." But the question is, in what way does the sacramental mode modify our concept of "presence here," while leaving intact the basic common-sense meaning of the latter?

However difficult it may be to answer this question positively, certain solutions may be rejected because they do not leave intact the common-sense meaning of "presence here." They modify too radically the concept so that it is no longer such as to permit us to state that what is on the altar *is* Christ. And this is the ultimate criterion, for Christ said of what he held in his hands: "This *is* my body." This was a common-sense statement, however wonderful; and it must be understood primarily in a common-sense way.

One solution which is inadequate would attribute spiritual omni-presence to the glorified body of Christ. Now, whatever be the meaning of such an assertion (Fr. Karl Rahner develops this difficult and much disputed notion in his writings on death, [3]) it is clear that it is irrelevant to the problem of the Eucharist. For such a presence would have no particular relation to the elements placed upon the altar, and there would be no more reason to affirm Christ's presence in them than to affirm it elsewhere. Or, if a special relationship is postulated with the sacraments, then it does not appear how any distinction could be made between the Eucharist and the rest.

Nor is it sufficient to explain Christ's presence as realized by mere symbolism. On this point, I think, all Catholic theologians would be agreed, although, as will be seen in the following chapters, much depends on what meaning is given to the word "symbolism." The encyclical, *Mysterium fidei,*

---

2. That sacramental presence of Christ does depend on faith, I have atempted to show elsewhere, in the tradition of St. Augustine and St. Thomas; cf. *Meeting Christ in the Sacraments,* 91 ff. The question is fully developed from the historical point of view by L. Villette, *Foi et sacrement,* Paris, vol. I, 1959; vol. II, 1964.

3. *Zur Theologie des Todes* (Quaestiones Disputatae, n. 2), Freiburg i. B., 1958.

with the normal—and Scholastic—meaning in mind, devoted five paragraphs to this point, obviously with the current theological situation in view.[4] How far this insistence touched on the real problem is a matter which will be considered later. This much is clear already: it is necessary to define with some precision the role played by symbolism (understood in the normal acceptation) in the sacrament.

The encyclical develops the traditional theme of the symbolism of bread and wine in relation to the unity of the Church. But this symbolism, it is noted, while "it helps us to understand the effect produced by this sacrament, the unity of the mystical body, at the same time does not reveal the nature of the sacrament, by which it is distinguished from the rest." [5]

In thus restricting its explanation of Eucharistic symbolism to the effect of the sacrament the encyclical is perhaps guilty of over-simplification, even on the ground it has chosen, for it seems clear that what is seen as bread and wine is also the symbol of Christ himself, the food come down from heaven. It is precisely through the medium of this symbol that Christ is made present.

This is the case in the other sacraments, and the very concept of a sacrament requires that this be so in the Eucharist also. It is just the problem of the Eucharistic presence that, within the symbol of himself Christ is truly and substantially made present. [6] In whatever explanation is given of this, the realm of "mere symbolism" must ultimately be transcended. At the same time it must be taken into account. The whole Church is a sacrament or efficacious symbol of Christ; the Eucharist belongs to this sacrament and, while symbolizing Christ, procures his presence in the Church.

But how can a symbol transcend mere symbolism? We must believe that it does, insists the encyclical. [7] Taught by Christ, we must say of this symbol what we cannot say of any other: This *is* his body. A symbol of which we affirm that it is identified with what it signifies: the paradox is so striking that the Church, to defend and expose her teaching, could hardly have avoided the task of making more explicit its formulation. This she has done in the dogma of transubstantiation. In this some attempt is made to give a positive meaning to the notion of sacramental "presence here."

---

4. § § 40-44 (*Acta Ap. Sed.*, 57 [1965], 764-765).
5. § 44 (*Acta Ap. Sed.*, loc. cit., 765).
6. This seems clearly to be the burden of John 6, taken as a whole; for, whatever may be the opinion of biblical scholars as to the sources of the chapter, there is some significance to be seen in the actual juxtaposition of the parts.
7. § 45 (*Acta Ap. Sed.*, loc. cit., 766).

5

TRANSUBSTANTIATION

The term "transubstantiation" first makes its appearance in theological writings in the middle of the twelfth century. As a way for expressing how Christ is made present by the Eucharistic consecration it has been adopted by a succession of general councils (Lateran IV, Lyons II, Trent). The Council of Trent described it as a "most suitable" expression for referring to "that wonderful and unique change of the whole substance of the bread into the body, and of the whole substance of the wine into the blood, only the species of the bread and wine remaining unaffected." [1]

The problem being discussed by modern theologians is: what does the term really mean? As long as Scholastic philosophy, in one form or another, provided the framework of Catholic theological thought there was fairly general agreement on interpretation. This was possible because, in the context of this philosophy, the term "substance," together with its correlative "accident," possesses a specific and agreed mean-

---

1. Trent, sess. 13, can. 2 on the Eucharist (Denzinger-Schönmetzer 1652).

ing. Then it was said that after the consecration all that is perceptible to the senses in the bread and wine remains unchanged (the "accidents"), while the "substance"—what makes an existing thing to be what it is—is changed into the body and blood of Christ. [2]

This placid state of affairs no longer exists, for Scholastic philosophy no longer enjoys undisputed sway in Catholic theological schools. There appear to be two broad reasons for this.

Firstly, the revelations of modern science have raised serious doubts, even among Scholastic thinkers, as to the legitimacy of applying to other than spiritual beings the Scholastic concept of "substance." For, while the continuity of self-consciousness would seem to legitimize the use of the idea for personal beings, the account given of the world by the experimental sciences appears to exclude any possibility of finding a meaningful sense in which the idea might be employed for non-spiritual beings. The difficulty appears all the more obvious when it is question of artificial constructs such as bread. For nowadays even the most devoted Scholastic could hardly subscribe to the simple medieval view that a piece of bread or a cup of wine is a single "substance;" modern chemistry and physics would at the very least seem to demand from him the admission that bread and wine are conglomerations of more elemental "substances." Several neo-Scholastics would prefer to dispense with the notion of "substance" altogether in these cases.

There is a second reason for uneasiness about Scholastic philosophy and it is closely linked with an awareness of the transcendence of the word of God. It does not seem legitimate to bind the theological exposition of this word to any particular philosophy. The most that can be hoped for from any human system of thought is that it will provide insights for men of a particular period in history into the divine plan of salvation. At the present time, it is argued, the categories of Scholastic thought are no longer meaningful; it is for theologians to undertake the task of reformulating the Christian message in terms which speak to modern man. For this, it is urged, the approach of existential phenomenology is the only one suitable.

In the current discussion of the Eucharist it is the interpretation based on existential phenomenology which has carried the day, both with those who explicitly propose the adoption of this philosophy and with some of those who are discontented with the Scholastic concept of material "substance."

THE PHENOMENOLOGICAL APPROACH

Phenomenology, while it is often described as simply a method, is in fact an independent philosophy for it is based on a particular theory of knowledge—and one that is not a little difficult. [3] Emerging as a reaction against the positivism of the experimental sciences (their tendency, that is, to exclude any form of knowledge not acquired by their own, experimental method), phenomenology directs attention to the subject's experience of the world and proceeds by a detailed description of this experience. There is more to knowledge than what the scientists report, but this "more" does not consist in a mirror-image of "reality." To claim that it does is to abandon experience; subject and object may not be divorced in this fashion. Knowledge is the immediate presence

---

2. No attempt is made here to explain the traditional account of transubstantiation, which may easily be found elsewhere.

3. Useful introductions, written by a theist: William A. Luijpen, *Phenomenology and Metaphysics,* Pittsburgh-Louvain, 1965; idem, *Phenomenology and Atheism,* Pittsburgh-Louvain, 1964; for criticism of Fr. Luijpen's earlier work, see D. M. De Petter, "Een geamendeerde Phenomenologie," *Tijdschrift voor Philosophie,* 22 (1960), 286-306.

of the thinking subject to a present reality, so that subject and meaning are inseparable, one implying the other. It is absurd to speak of "things-in-themselves," things without man. Man is always presupposed; and all that I can speak of is the "in-itself-for-me."

While a certain uneasiness about possible idealistic tendencies in such a theory of knowledge is understandable, this does not seem sufficient reason for denying the phenomenologist's basic assertion that meaning implies a subject and that for me reality is what I know. And on the basis of this assertion a description of reality centred on man may legitimately be built up.

Because of its interest in man, existential phenomenology has undoubtedly shown itself capable of drawing attention to aspects of the human situation neglected by other philosophies, including Scholasticism. For this reason many theologians have used its categories in their efforts to restate the Christian message. It is my own opinion, whatever reservations I shall later make, that they have proved the legitimacy and the value of their undertaking.

What is particularly relevant to sacramental theology is the phenomenological approach to signs. Theological analysis of sacramental signs has been in the past very largely based on a purely gnoseological or "information" theory of sign; that is to say, on a notion of sign as a medium of intellectual knowledge, as a signal pointing to a reality outside itself.

Phenomenologists have drawn attention to symbol-making as an activity of man, in which man expresses himself, in which, indeed, he truly humanizes himself. This concept is closely allied with that of man's corporeal condition. Far from being the prison of man's soul, the body is the subject himself, the medium through which he realizes his presence in space and time. It is through a like medium that others make themselves present to the subject. The symbol-making of man is a development of their corporeity, a means of inter-personal communication, at all levels at which such communication can be realized.

The central place assigned to man in the phenomenological theory of knowledge is easily recognized in the phenomenological description of symbol-making. It is what man makes of things which is important. "Brute reality"—the thing-in-itself—may possess a meaning for the experimental sciences. Man as such, however, can name things and give them a meaning far removed from their physico-chemical composition. True enough, the Greek mind, which has exercised such a formative influence on modern Western man, allied itself with the sciences and attempted to reduce knowledge to logical affirmations about "brute reality." But this is pure empiricism and must be overcome, particularly if, as Christians and theologians, we wish to recapture the world of the Hebrew authors of the Scriptures. For they were not interested in empirical nature. For them reality was significant in so far as it could be assumed into their existential situation. This was what their affirmations were about, not about "brute reality."

Phenomenologists would prefer not to talk about "substance," a typical Greek category, having no relevance to the dynamism of the human situation. But if they are forced to use the term—perhaps because they are theologians and wish to respect the teaching of the Church—they interpret it in a new way.

The Hebrew, says one non-Catholic theologian, because of his faith, could discover in the reality offered to his senses a more substantial reality, related to the will of God. For the Hebrew of the Bible seeks beyond "brute reality," listening for what things say, the will they express, the "word" they translate. "The substance of a reality is in the divine intention which is realized in it." And then transubstantiation will not be a physical change, but will depend on God's will. [4]

---

4. Cf. F.-J. Leenhardt, *Ceci est mon corps* ("Cahiers théologiques" n. 37), Neuchâtel-Paris, 1955, pp. 27 ff.

A preliminary comment on this phenomenological view may be inserted at this point for the sake of clarity. Though the system has proved itself capable, as in the example just noted, of assimilating traditional theological terms, it interprets these in a wholly new way. And this becomes clear if it is observed that phenomenology is based on an "either-or." It takes account of, and admits, only two kinds of knowledge: that of the experimental sciences and that of the phenomenological reduction. The first being eliminated as far as authentically human and therefore theological thinking is concerned, the only true form of human and theological thinking must renounce interest in the "thing-in-itself," in "brute reality." Either empiricism or the "in-itself-for-me" is the only option left. The "for-me" is the trick—if that word may be used—of the whole system.

In this man-centeredness lies the strength, the usefulness and, I believe, the weakness of the phenomenological approach. The consequences of the "for-me" are enormous. For most philosophers the final consequence is atheism. Catholic theologians who adopt the system argue, evidently, that this is not necessary. Our concern will be to study what the "either-or" makes of the mystery of the Eucharist.

The first problem for Catholic theologians is, naturally, the teaching of the Council of Trent. In the present climate of reappraisal and theorizing theologians have been compelled to examine the acts of the Council in an effort to discover what precisely was defined by the conciliar Fathers when they spoke of transubstantiation.

THE COUNCIL OF TRENT

No attempt will be made here to follow the detailed, positive studies of Trent which have recently appeared. Nor is this necessary; for the view according to which the Council incorporated Scholastic philosophy into the Church's dogma as something to be believed could not be seriously maintained today by anyone; and certainly no argument resting on such an assertion could gain a hearing today.

The results of historical research are not unanimous as to what the Fathers of Trent really did intend to define.[5] What does emerge clearly from the studies made is that Trent's teaching does not impose on believers the obligation of formulating

---

5. Fr. E. H. Schillebeeckx has presented a close study of the acts of Trent in *Tijdschrift voor theologie,* 5 (1965), 136-172; S. maintains that the Fathers of Trent, though they thought in Aristotelian (Scholastic) categories, intended to define dogmatically the reality characteristic of the Eucharistic presence, and not the categories which they employed in their discussions and their formula.

The solution does not lack subtlety and is, presumably, dependent on the notion of dogma outlined elsewhere by Fr. Schillebeeckx; cf. his articles, "Het begrip waarheid" and "Het niet-begrippelijk kenmoment in onze Godskennis volgens Thomas van Aquino," in *Theologische peilingen,* Deel I: *Openbaring en theologie,* Bilthoven, 1964, pp. 85-232. Adopting the theory of his teacher, Fr. D. De Petter, S. makes what he admits is a fine distinction, in a dogmatic formula, between the essential kernel of the dogmatic affirmation and the adventitious mode of expression given it. One obviously implies the other, but the true value of the definition is found in the accurate perspectives opened up on divine reality by the concepts used. Through them, imperfect though they are, in virtue of a non-conceptual moment in our knowledge we "in-tend" the divine truth (op. cit., p. 198). The theory is contrasted with that of Fr. Maréchal and his school (including Fr. K. Rahner) which falls back on the non-intellectual dynamic of the human spirit towards the infinite in their explanation of our knowledge of God. Both theories appeal to a "projection" of human concepts onto divine truth, but Fr. De Petter, followed by Fr. Schillbeeckx, insisits that this must have an objective justification, missing in the Maréchal opinion. – Other historical studies of Trent: Rahner, "Die Gegenwart Christi im Sakrament des Herrenmahles," in *Schriften zur Theologie,* Bd. IV, Einsiedeln etc., 1960, pp. 357-385; E. Gutwenger, "Substanz und Akzidenz in der Eucharistielehre," *Zeitschrift für katholische Theologie,* 83 (1961), 257-306.

their belief in the real presence in terms of Aristotelian or Scholastic philosophy.

Even if one justly refuses any attempt radically to relativize dogmatic statements, one is at liberty to interpret the term "transubstantiation" in concepts not specifically those of Scholasticism —provided, however, that one does not betray the meaning of the Council. This is equivalent to saying that there is a legitimate possibility for theologians to propose new interpretations of the term "substance"; but it is for them to show that in doing so they have not abandoned the direction in which the Council of Trent was pointing.

Possibly this may sound very much like saying in a rather roundabout way that theologians may propose any interpretation provided that it is in the long run identical with that of Scholasticism, since it is fairly certain that the spirit of Trent was predominantly Scholastic. I should prefer not to formulate the matter in that way; and this not for any purely diplomatic reasons, in order to avoid alienating non-Scholastics; but because it seems to me that it is not correct to interpret any conciliar document from the prejudiced position of a particular philosophy. One can only appeal, so far as stating dogma is concerned, to that common-sense which is prior to philosophizing and which transcends the philosophical systems both of the conciliar Fathers and of individual members of the faithful.

What I would propose, then, is that no more specific dogmatic signification may be attached to the terms employed by Trent than that which they possess in their pre-philosophic, common-sense usage. It was in this fashion that the term "substantial presence" was interpreted in the preceding chapter, relying on a comparison of the various modes of Christ's presence in the Church; and good reasons appear to impose a like solution here.

In the first place, it will be noted that the encyclical, *Mysterium fidei,* speaks of the "dogma of transubstantiation."[6] In so far as a notion of substance is implied here it would seem clear that what is dogmatically defined in Trent's statement cannot involve acceptance or imposition of any particular system of philosophy. It does not in the least imply despair of the possibility of reaching philosophical certitude in certain areas to admit a field of legitimate doubt concerning the value of any system, Scholastic or otherwise.

There is, of course, a number of philosophical positions—for example, the affirmation of man's immortality—which is presupposed by revelation. But the same certitude does not attach either to a system or to the fashion in which a truth presupposed by revelation is incorporated into a system. Consequently, whatever a theologian's personal philosophical convictions may be, he is bound to concede liberty to other believers in their attempt at expressing with the aid of philosophical concepts the defined statements of the Church. He certainly is not entitled to protest simply because their interpretations conflict with his chosen philosophy.

The concept of "substance," then, as used in the Eucharistic definitions, cannot be identified with the concept found in Aristotelianism, Thomism, or any other system. Dogmatic definitions must have a more universal basis than that.

Along the same line of thought, it would further appear that it is only by appealing to pre-philosophical notions that an acceptable sense may be given to those paragraphs of *Mysterium fidei* which concern rules of speaking in theology. [7] It has been these paragraphs which have been the particular object of attack by those who considered that the encyclical illegitimately imposed Aristotelian philosophy on the Church. Such fears, I suggest, may be seen, from the encyclical itself, to be groundless. It could hardly have been made plainer in

---

6. § 10 (*Acta Ap. Sed.*, 57 [1965], 755); cf. § 54, quoting Pius VI (loc. cit., 768).

7. § § 23-25 (loc. cit., 757-758).

the text that, in refusing to permit the rejection of traditional dogmatic formulas, the appeal was being made to pre-philosophical human experience.

These formulas, states the encyclical, express concepts which are not tied to any particular civilization or stage of scientific development or theological school. On the contrary, they signify what the human mind perceives of things "by necessary and universal experience." [8]

Appeal is being made to ideas and judgments which man forms through no other experience than that of being human. These are ideas such as "person," "nature," and judgments concerning one's own existence and that of the world. It is the work of philosophy to explore these ideas and judgments; and the history of philosophy demonstrates how widely divergent man's thinking about them can be. But at the stage of pre-philosophic experience every man forms these ideas and these judgments for himself. It is man, and his ability to know, which the Church is defending when she claims that such experience is necessary and universal. If it were not, not only would the pastoral office of the Church be frustrated; there could be no communication between men. That certain philosophies criticize adversely this pre-philosophic experience of man is a fact; and the question is one to which we shall have to return.

That the words used to express such common-sense ideas and judgments are arbitrary symbols is too obvious to state, for this is the condition of all human language. But there is an agreed pre-philosophic signification to the words people of any particular language-group commonly use. Though, as has been said, the Church cannot avoid modifying language if she is to give linguistic expression to her mysteries, she still makes use of words according to their basic, commonly-agreed signification. Nothing more than this, it seems to me, is implied in the encyclical's claim that dogmatic formulas, in so far as they refer to necessary and universal experience, are meaningful to all men, of all times, of all places.[9]

It is because dogmatic formulas are phrased in terms signifying notions of necessary and universal experience that they may not be rejected. For it is just the characteristic of such notions that there is nothing to replace them. Clearly, the very fact that these are notions drawn from human experience implies the vast gulf lying between them and the divine truth to which they give expression. And, consequently, other aspects of revelation, not touched upon in the dogmatic formulas, may be discovered or brought into the consciousness of the Church. Clearly, too, as the encyclical itself points out,[10] further light may be thrown on the formulas themselves when the pre-philosophic notions they express are developed according to the methods proper to theology.

But neither the indication of new aspects nor the more profound penetration of defined dogmas involves rejection of the original formula. For this, however inadequate it must be in terms of its object, the divine reality, is still "adequate" from the point of view of man's knowing the divine reality. "Adequate" does not mean here "complete" or "exhaustive"; it simply means "accurate" or "pointing in the right direction." Concretely, the dogmatic proposition serves to formulate that judgment of the believer by which, through faith, he truly attains the divine reality. This is to say that whatever added perfection is later brought to the conceptualization of the mystery, one essential criterion by which claims to new insights are evaluated is the dogmatic formula itself.

There is no difficulty about admitting the existence in dogmatic formulas of "mythological" elements (the scriptural

---

8. § 24 (loc. cit., 758).
9. § 24 (loc. cit., 758).
10. § 25 (loc. cit., 758).

and credal account of the Ascension comes immediately to mind). These derive from images and thought-patterns which are traceable to historical and cultural influences. By definition they do not belong to "necessary and universal experience." But, if language means anything at all, within such historically-conditioned formulations there must be an area where appeal *is* made to "necessary and universal experience" as a human basis for true statements about the divine economy.

Philosophical *systems* are introduced into the formulation of revelation only at a phase of thought subsequent to that to which dogmatic formulas belong; it is then that systematic theology of one kind or another begins; and consequently changes in philosophical fashion or in popularly-developed world-views leave unaffected the validity of the Church's dogmatic statements. It is, however, clear that this understanding of dogma will prove unacceptable to anyone who, for philosophical reasons, either rejects the validity of common sense or refuses to acknowledge its metaphysical implications. To this difficulty we must now turn.

THE LIMITS OF PHENOMENOLOGY

It would, of course, be naive to imagine that philosophical systems refrain from comment on man's pre-philosophical notions and judgments. To the extent that the Church is bound to safe-guard the human basis of her teaching-office she must be committed to a certain philosophy of man and his environment. It might better be said that this is a negative philosophy to the extent that it involves, rather than a constructed system, the rejection of any philosophy contradicting the necessary presuppositions of faith. A positive view of man (primarily, as one who is *able to receive* revelation) is implicit in this negative attitude. Such approval as the Church has given the philosophy of St. Thomas says no more essentially than that this system in no way contradicts these necessary presuppositions and has proved itself capable of constructing a synthesis on this basis. Any philosophy that could do as much would, presumably, be equally welcome to the Church.

It is here that the question of the acceptability of phenomenology within the Catholic faith must be raised. That its man-centred interest has proved itself capable of bringing new insights to theology has already been willingly granted. The decisive question about the system as a whole, however, is whether the theory of knowledge on which it is based comes at any point into conflict with the necessary pre-philosophic presuppositions which the Church must make if revelation is to have any meaningful sense for man.

The formulation of this question will make it clear that I think a distinction may validly be made between certain conclusions reached by theologians using the phenomenological method and the epistemological theory on which the system is based. The consideration of the meaning reality has for the thinking subject appears to be a completely valid and revealing approach to created reality and to certain areas, at least, of revelation (or, to be more accurate, to the believer's reaction to revelation). The acquisitions of this approach in sacramentology, for example, have undoubtedly advanced this part of theology.

But if this is a legitimate manner of viewing reality, I am not prepared to admit that it constitutes the only manner. Or, more exactly, I suggest that there are elements within this manner of viewing reality which are systematically ignored by phenomenologists; and I am not prepared to accept this element of system. And it will be my contention that the Church is not prepared to accept it either; again, not because she is imposing any other philosophical system, but because she is bound to defend certain pre-philosophic suppositions if she is to fulfill her saving mission.

What is, on principle, ignored by phenomenology is that reality, in manifesting itself to me as "for me," at the same time manifests itself as *independent of me.* Nor is it merely the object of the natural sciences which manifests its independence. The "either-or" of phenomenology—either the positive knowledge given by the experimental sciences or the phenomenological reduction—does not impose itself. One proof of this is that, in fact, many philosophers are satisfied that there is a further dimension to human knowledge; a fact which, in itself, disposes of the "either-or" as a necessary alternative. Here I think it is sufficient to appeal to the common-sense judgment that things exist independently of the thinking subject and that one thing is different from another.

Clearly, if I am informed by a scientist of other aspects of reality, not apparent to me in my common-sense judgment, I am willing to accede (at least hypothetically) to his specialized knowledge and to correct, so far as I am able, my common-sense appreciation of the structure of the world—but not to the extent of denying my own immediate and intuitive encounter with reality as existing independently of me. For human knowledge is broader than the specialized scientific view, and broader too than the artificial "either-or" of phenomenology.

Revelation confirms and develops this common-sense judgment with its doctrine of creation which indicates the Trinitarian ground of the independence which I attribute to the things I know. And, setting aside the possibility of a metaphysical affirmation of creation, as a believer I am compelled to affirm what common-sense judges for itself. [11]

Here, I submit, is to be found the common-sense meaning of "substance." It would be better if the word were approached with all notions from the history of philosophy banished from the mind, for undoubtedly its complex history has given it an unenviable reputation. It is simply that when I affirm that a thing manifests itself to me as having certain characteristics and as enjoying independent existence, I implicitly affirm that it is a "substance" (or conglomeration of "substances," if there are reasons for putting it that way). Or, in theological terms, what issues from creation enjoying a particular form of independent existence is a substance.

It must be insisted once again: only common sense is being appealed to. There is no question of ancient, medieval or modern cosmologies regarding the structure of the world. No system of philosophy, as such, is involved. Put technically, the claim is being made that the "either-or" of phenomenology is inadequate because it rejects metaphysics. But that way of putting it may already introduce confusion since phenomenologists are inclined to use the word "ontological" with reference to the "in-itself-for-me"; and it is just this that does violence to what might be called the "in-itself-for-me-as-manifesting-its-independence-of-me."

The Church cannot, in the fashion advocated by the Barthian school, content herself with the preaching of the word of God. The word comes to men; and this implies that they can receive it. So, unless the Church is content to proclaim a timeless truth having no bearing on the lives of men, she must defend man himself—often from himself. She must defend his natural powers of knowledge, even while acknowledging his sin and while preaching a salvation which comes from God alone. It is here that she cannot renounce the common-sense idea of "substance," that she must maintain

---

11. This last is an *ad-hominem* argument, for belief in creation would be irrational if it were not *possible* to affirm the existence of God. This is the theological, as distinct from the apologetic, significance of the teaching of Vatican I, Dogmatic Const., *Dei Filius,* on Catholic faith, ch. 2 (Denzinger-Schönmetzer, 3004).

(if in other words) that in my existential encounter with reality I recognize the independent being of the world.

TRANSUBSTANTIATION

Along the lines of the common-sense interpretation here proposed the "dogma of transubstantiation" presents no very complicated concept. It simply states in pre-philosophic terms, what must be postulated if Christ's words, *This is my body, my blood,* are to be verified for faith; namely, the whole substance of the bread must be changed into Christ's body, the whole substance of the wine into his blood.

What the dogma states is no more than what is required if Christ's words, as spoken at the Last Supper and at Mass, are to be understood as referring to the thing placed on the table or contained in the cup. For, at the pre-philosophical level of common sense, "substance" is that which permits us to state that a thing existing independently of ourselves, our knowledge or our attitudes, is either bread or the body of Christ. And it is apparent to common sense that a thing understood this way may not be simultaneously bread and the body of Christ. By her dogmatic statement the Church makes clear the sense in which she reads the scriptural report of Christ's words at the Last Supper: the word "is" indicates, as a result of Christ's power, real identity between what lay on the table and his body. (Apart from stating the the whole Christ is contained under each species, even after separation of the parts, the dogmatic statement does not further clarify the terms "body" and "blood.") It could be argued that the dogma is no more than a verbal clarification of Christ's statement within the context of a realist epistemology. But even if it is considered to be a conclusion drawn from belief in the truth of Christ's words, it is so immediately apparent to common sense that its affirmation is unavoidable.

Verbally, this statement of the dogma may appear to coincide with the Scholastic elaboration of the nature of the Eucharistic change. But this is so only because Scholasticism claims to have analyzed and refined common-sense experience and therefore retains for its strictly philosophical concepts the same terms as those used to designate the fundamental concepts of common sense. It is the latter which are incorporated into the dogma, not the former.[12]

---

12. In the foregoing explanation the term "transubstantiation" is taken to refer to a real (or ontological) change demanded by the Eucharistic presence as revealed in the Scriptures and interpreted by the Church. Fr. Schillebeeckx (art. cit., *Worship*, 40 [1966], 324-328), on the contrary, suggests that the notion of "transubstantiation" constitutes a manner of presenting the dogma of real change at the level of a philosophy of nature; the real change, he proposes, should be termed *transentatio*. I believe such a distinction to be an unnecessary and confusing complication, raising the question as to just how Fr. Schillebeeckx conceives of "substance." In any case, I have explained transubstantiation itself as *transentatio*. This appears to be the only way to account for the encyclical's insistence on the perennial validity of the notion of transubstantiation, which Fr. Schillebeeckx appears to consider out of date. Then too, the level of natural philosophy is not reached until an explanation of the "substance" of material reality is offered in some such terms as those of the Scholastic hylemorphic theory. The theology of the Eucharist does not require the introduction of any such problematic speculation, precisely because the dogma postulates a change of the *whole* substance of bread and wine. See also E. Schillebeeckx, "Die eucharistische wijze van Christus werkelijke tegenwoordigheid," *Tijdschrift voor Theologie*, 6 (1966), 359-394, which appeared after the present text was written. Here S. uses the term "transubstantiation" in reference to "reality" (*werkelijkheid*) which is distinguished from "reality as appearing" (*als verschijnend; het fenomenale*) (p. 390). The former is affirmed as given, it would seem, in virtue of divine creative activity (p. 389). It appears to me, on a first reading, that an implicit appeal is being made here to the common-sense notion of "substance." — A German translation of S' articles on the Eucharist has recently been published: *Die eucharistische Gegenwart*, Düsseldorf, 1967.

The fundamentally positive character of the Church's intervention in the Eucharistic debate should be underlined. The phenomenological approach is not condemned. There is simply renewed insistence on the minimum requirements of a philosophy that claims right of entry into the sphere of the word of God preached by the Church. And this can only clarify the problem of modern theology regarding the possibility of adopting new categories. It is for theologians to demonstrate the value of such categories by using them successfully.

But the Church must safeguard her message. And she does so, in the case of the Eucharist, by demanding that the independent reality of things be recognized. If phenomenology ignores this aspect of reality, then theologians must modify phenomenology. The effect is not destructive but synthetic; the possibility is left open of integrating the values affirmed by phenomenology into a more fully human outlook. Only if divine revelation is conceived of as totally irrelevant to man as an intelligent being will this kind of intervention by the Church be considered intrusive. The fact is, it matters what man thinks about revelation; this is his dignity as one made in the image of God, as one whose judgments about reality do not have to be suppressed in the face of the word of God, as one who finds in that word the unsuspected and wholly unmerited fulfillment of himself.

I have thought it preferable to state briefly my own position as clearly as possible before developing more fully the phenomenological theory of the Eucharist. It is as well that readers be aware of the point of view from which this theory is being presented. Nevertheless, an attempt is made in the following chapter to offer an objective account of the new theory. In this way it may prove possible to determine whether, and to what degree, a realist understanding of the Eucharist may be complemented by the phenomenological approach.

6

A PHENOMENOLOGY OF THE EUCHARIST

The position now reached in our argument may be summarized as follows. The defined teaching of the Church requires that we admit such change in the bread and wine of the Eucharist as will permit us to state, on the basis of a common-sense judgment, that after the consecration the things placed on the altar are the body and blood of Christ. In common-sense terms this involves a substantial change in bread and wine; and this is transubstantiation.

I have argued that this common-sense judgment implies that reality immediately manifests itself to me as existing with its own characteristics, independently of me, and that it is this aspect of reality which is signified by the term "substance." It is under this aspect that reality manifests the creative activity of God; and it is at this level that the Church locates the change known as transubstantiation.

It has already been pointed out that this interpretation of common-sense experience is either rejected or overlooked by radical phenomenologists. It is clear, then, that theologians who adopt phenomenology without making the criticism that has been made here will be compelled to seek another interpretation of the term "substance" and, consequently, of "transubstantiation." It should perhaps be repeated that in itself such an effort of reinterpretation is quite legitimate within theology. It is only if the implications of a radically phenomenological approach are worked out that it becomes possible to place the new view of the Eucharist within the context of the full Christian outlook and so to judge how far it is in harmony with other beliefs of the Church and with the common-sense judgments which these beliefs presuppose.

The dogma of transubstantiation is not being attacked by the phenomenological theologians. They affirm their belief in the real presence and are prepared to accept Trent's teaching. This point must be insisted upon if injustice is not to be done to a group of theologians whose pastoral concern is patent. The whole discussion turns on the meaning of "substance"; and even if one considers the phenomenological interpretation inadequate, one is not entitled to impugn the good faith and the theological enterprsie of those who have attempted to restate the doctrine of the Eucharist.

THEORY

For the sake of clarifying the issues, the problem has just been stated in its most critical form. In fact, true to their phenomenological background, the new theologians prefer to approach the matter from a more descriptive angle. As their writings are not easily accessible, a fairly full account of the way in which one of them argues will be useful. [1]

We must begin, argues Fr. Smits, not with the notion of transubstantiation, but with the concrete event of the Last Supper and of the Mass. At the Last Supper the Jews who heard the words of Jesus could not have understood him to be making some distinction, unintelligible for them, between spirit and matter and then (with regard to matter) between body and blood. For them, his words (twice repeated in the parallel style of the Hebrews) meant simply: This is myself who am going to suffer for you.

The apostles would have understood this as a fulfillment of the Old Alliance with whose forms they were familiar. They would have realized that Christ was choosing a New People and was entering into a New Alliance with them. Through the symbol of bread and wine he was establishing this New Alliance; and it was his will that the Alliance should be preserved through repetition of the meal.

It was a question, then, of the bond between Christ and his Church: even when he would be absent, the serving of the bread and wine would provide a means through which he could give himself totally to his people. In these circumstances, it is no longer legitimate for us to speak of bread and wine. To do so would be to fail to understand that Christ wills to give, not bread and wine, but himself. This is precisely the content of the New Alliance: he gives himself to us totally (and not just his body). We must then give ourselves to him totally so that we are his people. The level at which all this happens is that of inter-personal relations; it is a question of expressing friendship through a gift.

---

1. Cf. Luchesius Smits, O.F.M. Cap., *Actuele vragen rondom de transsubstantiatie en de tegenwoordigheid des Heren in de H. Eucharistie,* Roermond, 1965. This is the fullest Catholic account of the new approach. Most of the articles written in Holland were published in lesser-known catechetical and devotional reviews and in newspapers; cf. *Ephemerides Theologicae Lovanienses,* 41 (1965), 305-306 (Bulletin, reproducing part of a letter of Fr. P. Schoonenberg); and E. Schillebeeckx, *Worship,* 40 (1966), 330, nn. 15, 16, 17, for more exact references to articles (*De Heraut,* noted there, is *De Heraut van het Heilig Hart*). See also F.-J Leenhardt, op. cit. (ch. 5, n. 4); M. Thurian, *L'Eucharistie,* Neuchâtel-Paris, 1963[2], pp. 259-278; C. Davis, "The Theology of Transubstantiation" *Sophia* (Melbourne, Australia), April, 1964, 12-24 (cf. ch. 1, n. 2, above, for correspondence in *The Tablet* [London]).

In this notion of expressed friendship Fr. Smits believes that he has found the scriptural concept of the Eucharist. This he proceeds to analyze according to the phenomenological method in order to show that it does indeed involve a "transubstantiation."

To begin with, Christ as man used material things, as other men do, as an extension of his bodiliness, as a means of expressing himself in the material world. So, the hostess, for example, offers her guests coffee and cakes. Afternoon coffee sipped by a group of friends is not meant primarily to have any nutritive value. The food offered expresses the hostess's friendship for her guests; and by accepting what is offered the guests accept and reciprocate this friendship.

More striking still is the example of the violinist. Perhaps as a speaker he is inarticulate, incapable of expressing to others what kind of person he is. But when he plays his violin the true person suddenly appears. The instrument becomes part of him, a development of his corporeity, of himself, the only true means he has of communicating with others.

This is "incarnation" (in the phenomenological sense): the human spirit assuming control of matter and only in this way attaining its own perfection. It was in this way that Christ, as man, incarnated his human love in the bread and wine. But this is not yet transubstantiation.

Christ is also Son of God. In his humanity he expresses God's saving intent for mankind; and, consequently, in the gifts he offered us as man the love of the God-man for men is made incarnate. The difficulty here for the Western (as opposed to the Semitic) mind is, according to Fr. Smits, that we are almost inevitably drawn to think of a gift offered as a signal, pointing outside itself to the giver with his friendship for us. But this is not a true appreciation, as becomes clear if we consider signs (such as the giving of gifts) in their full dimensions as human actions. Then we realize that the event of friendship takes place in the sign itself. There is no other way for human love to realize itself. The sign that Christ gives the apostles is the incarnate love of the God-man. God's interiority (his saving design) is made incarnate in the humanity of Christ and in those material things which Christ adopts as an extension of his humanity.

What, then, we might well ask, are the gifts "in themselves?" This is, in the strictest sense, an irrelevant question for the phenomenologists, for it reveals that the questioner has not grasped the phenomenological approach but is still a victim of the "natural" (epistemological) attitude.

If we are going to think of the "body" of Christ as something distinct from his blood and from his soul, then we are similarly going to think of the bread and wine as ordinary food. This is the sort of approach a chemist would adopt; and certainly for him, should he get the opportunity to analyze them, the consecrated elements would reveal themselves as nothing more than bread and wine. On the contrary, if we think instead of human bodiliness—that is, man—as extended in gifts, then the bread and wine become *corpus mysticum* (in Latin in the text). For then there is *identity*: the gifts form a unity with the human body of Christ; gifts and body are united with the interiority of the God-man who so expresses here his self-giving-to-us that he is present here in his whole person.

Fr. Smits insists again and again that transubstantiation cannot properly be conceived of apart from the Incarnation of the Word. It seems clear that by this he means that the Incarnation and the Eucharist are *one and the same mystery*. This he can say (or, at least, imply) because he conceives of the Incarnation in dynamic fashion: his concern is with the *activity* of Christ as the expression in the world of the saving design of God. From this (existential) principle he goes on to stress the continuity, perceivable in these perspectives, between the humanity of Christ and the things Christ takes in his hands as extensions of his humanity. When this point of view is adopted and is considered as the only one adequate to the mystery, it is not difficult to understand that questions concerning the "nature" of the gifts "in themselves" are dismissed as totally irrelevant. Such questions have as little to do with the divine saving action in Christ as a question concerning the physical structure of Christ's body.

When Berengarius proposed that the Eucharist is a symbol or sign of Christ the Church rightly rejected his teaching. For, according to Fr. Smits, both Berengarius and his adversaries conceived of a sign as a signal, that is, something pointing to a reality outside itself, which it does not contain. The Church was bound to condemn such an explanation of the Eucharist, and to insist that something more is required.

Western theology, however, has misinterpreted the Church's legitimate demand for "something more." Theologians, lacking a personalist philosophy, have been misled into thinking that the only alternative to a symbolic presence of Christ is the form of presence characteristic, not of persons, but of things. This led to the traditional, post-medieval notion of the substance of Christ's body replacing the substance of the bread—"substance" in both cases here being understood in a material sense. All this was missing the point. The presence of Christ is that of a person; and it is realized among men primarily through the corporeity of Christ and, in dependence on this, through the material realities which Christ uses.

The use of the terms "transignification" and "transfinalization" by certain of Fr. Smits' associates (though not, so far as I am aware, by Fr. Smits himself) may, perhaps, now be clear. It is illegitimate for Scholastic theologians to reject these terms and what they represent on the basis of a Scholastic understanding of "signs" or "signification." What the phenomenological theologians are trying to do is, in fact, exactly the same as what Scholastic theologians are trying to do. Both schools are attempting to elaborate what they consider the common-sense notion of "substance" and "transubstantiation" in terms of their respective philosophical systems. For the phenomenologist "transignification" *is* "transubstantiation." He does not mean, as a Scholastic might too readily assume, that the Eucharistic change consists simply in the attribution to bread of a new "relation of signification"; these are not the categories in which he thinks. He sees in man's use of symbols an anthropological activity in which man's interiority becomes incarnate, so that the symbol-action really contains the man within itself. And if the man should also be God then it will be the divine Person who is made present in his human symbol-actions.

The Scholastic and the phenomenological approaches evidently differ radically. For the latter the common-sense notion of "the substance of bread" is to be interpreted in terms of bread's use and value for man. It is, in Fr. Davis's words, a "human object." It has not, that is to say, a distinctive nature and a unified reality; rather it is "a product of human action which has a structure as a whole, with reality, unity and intelligibility relating it to man, but which is not as a structured whole a physical substance, even though grouping and ordering material parts or ingredients that are physical substances." [2]

Likewise, for Fr. Schoonenberg bread has theological interest only in so far as it is taken up into the sphere of human values: it is food for man or (when, for example, offered as a gift) it can be expressive of human sentiments for other persons.

Just as much as the vast majority of Scholastics the phenomenological theologians reject as absurd the notion that the Eucharistic change could be a chemical one. It must take place at another level of reality than that open to experimental

---

2. Fr. Davis, it would appear, adopts an eclectic approach for he seems willing to concede the Scholastic concept of "substance" for the constituent elements of bread and wine, even though he considers this irrelevant for Eucharistic theology. A thorough-going phenomenologist would not admit as much.

investigation. The Scholastic notion of a change in the reality of the bread as it exists in itself is considered untenable. [3]

The only alternative, and the one to which phenomenology naturally directs attention, is that the change takes place at the level of bread as a "thing-for-me" or as a "human object." Christ "gives to this same set of physical substances a new meaning" (Fr. Davis). "Transubstantiation," Fr. Schoonenberg puts it, "through which Christ's body is made present in the symbol of bread, consists in this (*hierin bestaat*) that bread and wine acquire a new meaning and significance." This is "transignification" or "transfinalization": the new meaning and purpose and value which the bread and wine acquire for man when the efficatious words of consecration are spoken over them.

The bread is no longer bread because the signification of this material for man and its relation to man are changed, because the divine saving will is recognized in the action of Christ at the Last Supper. The bread becomes the body of Christ because the matter is now an outward manifestation of Christ (Fr. Davis). It is within the context of a person-to-person relationship that Christ thus makes himself present (Fr. Schoonenberg). We are in the same realm of thought as that of Fr. Smits with his "incarnation of the divine design."

COMMENT

The presentation of Catholic teaching found in the encyclical, *Mysterium fidei,* is brief in the extreme. The central comments are so brief that they may be quoted in full:

> When transubstantiation has taken place, the appearances of bread and wine acquire, beyond doubt, a new meaning and a new finality. They are no longer ordinary bread and ordinary drink, but the symbol of a sacred thing and the

> symbol of spiritual nourishment. But if they acquire a new significance and a new finality, it is because they contain a new "reality," which we justly call *ontological.* [4]

Transignification and transfinalization are here relegated to the realm of appearances, that is to say, to the realm of what does not undergo the kind of change which the Church considers to be the true change of the Eucharistic mystery.

Such secondary change as the appearances do undergo is brought about only because of the true Eucharistic change which takes place at the "ontological" level: because the appearances contain a new "reality." Through several paragraphs [5] justification for this distinction is adduced from the Fathers and from the teaching of the Church. The Fathers are shown to appeal to the distinction between what appears to the senses and what is held on faith. Even more significantly they are quoted as saying that the power which effects the Eucharistic change "is the same as that by which almighty God

---

3. The reasons given differ. Evidently, phenomenologists, in virtue of their system, exclude from consideration the level of reality at which Scholastics – and, I have argued, the Church – place the change. Fr. Davis and his supporters in *The Tablet* are not so radical, nor so logical. The evidence of physical science convinces them that bread is not a substance but a conglomeration of substances (in the Scholastic sense). Since Trent teaches that it is *bread* which changes (and not the substances from which it is constituted) there is no point in considering possible changes at the level of the constituent substances. The problem here raised is hardly novel and has been widely discussed. To graft on to a Scholastic metaphysics, which one admits, the anti-metaphysical "ontology" of phenomenology, if not entirely self-contradictory, means that one renounces the realist interpretation of the real presence for a reason which, even according to one's own principles, is not compelling. I cannot believe that this line of thought will win many adherents.

4. § 46 (*Acta Ap. Sed.*, 57 [1965], 766).

5. § § 47-55 (loc. cit., 766-768).

created all things from nothing at the beginning of time." [6]

Is the new theory excluded by this section of the encyclical? The answer would seem to be that the encyclical is concerned only with restating, with the appropriate justification, the dogma of Trent. This statement is obviously not made in a theological vacuum; some, at least, of the writings that we have considered provide the context in which it is made. But the fact that a clarification of official teaching was judged to be necessary cannot in itself be interpreted as a condemnation of the new theory. What the encyclical does is to call attention to the criterion of orthodoxy against which any theory must be measured. The matter reverts to the theological interpretation of Trent, already discussed in the preceding chapter.

It does not appear to me that Fr. Smits would find anything opposed to his theory in the encyclical's relegation of transignification and transfinalization to the order of appearances and in its accompanying demand for a more profound or ontological change. I think he might object that the encyclical somewhat arbitrarily, if understandably, adopts the "Western" concept of sign—as signal— which he has argued is inadequate in the field of sacramental theology; and he would add that in these perspectives the encyclical is bound to postulate a deeper change.

But, then, Trent has already said as much; and Fr. Smits has no difficulty about explaining that the ontological change which Trent finds necessary is accounted for in his theory. It is, he says, when Christ takes bread into his hands, drawing it into the sphere of his own corporeity, that a truly ontological change takes place. Evidently, a Scholastic would reject this explanation as altogether too superficial and contrary to the plain sense of the encyclical; but a Scholastic cannot impose his own philosophical convictions on others in the name of *faith.*

I have already argued that the phenomenological "either-or" does violence to common sense. But possibly, now that the full force of the new position is seen, this claim begins to lose some of its cogency. If it is simply a matter of divergent philosophical opinions, it may be said at this point, why not leave the matter open, particularly because the phenomenological explanation has much to commend its personalistic bias? Again, I have argued that philosophical agnosticism of this kind does no credit to the human mind and *therefore* is dangerous to faith. But a more immediate appeal to faith itself may be more efficacious at this stage.

There is more in the encyclical than the judgment on the meaning of transignification and transfinalization. The "ontological" change required is explained further in terms which are strictly theological and which appeal to a revealed truth. "The power that effects this [change] is the same as that by which almighty God *created* all things from nothing at the beginning of time." [7] St. Ambrose is quoted:

> Could not the word of Christ, which is able to make from nothing what was not there before, change existing things into what they were not? For it is not of less account to give things new natures than to change natures. [8]

An affirmation is being made here that is of the highest significance both for the Christian life and for theology.

The believer can find here a very simple way of cutting through all the confusing discussion and making his own affirmation of faith. The level at which the creative and conserving action of God touches bread and wine (whatever these may be) is the level at which the Eucharistic change takes place. Clearly, bread and wine are products of human skill; they—

---

6. § 47; cf. § 51 (loc. cit.).
7. § 47 (loc. cit.); italics mine.
8. *De mysteriis,* 9, 50-52 (PL 16, 424); *Mysterium fidei,* § 51 (loc. cit.).

or their constitutive elements—are no less creatures holding their being from God. It is at this profound level of being where God gives these creatures their characteristic form of existence that he changes them so that what the priest holds in his hands *is* the body of Christ. What God now holds in existence, and what is contained in the unchanged appearances, is no longer bread but the body of Christ.

It will be observed that in this appeal to creation there is implicit an appeal to common sense, to that pre-philosophical affirmation of reality which is spontaneous and which is unaffected by subsequent judgments. For when we say that God creates the world we mean that he is the source of that being which we attribute to things when we affirm: This is a man; This is a tree; This is bread; This is the body of Christ.

The strictly theological problem is whether the phenomenological theory postulates a change in bread which is at the level of God's creative action. So far as I am aware, this problem has not been explicitly discussed by the theologians reviewed above. In fact, how a radical phenomenologist could discuss creation—or would want to—is inconceivable.

It would seem obvious that the new Eucharistic theory posits a purely anthropological change—one, that is, which depends solely on the use that man makes of things. For though, indeed, Fr. Smits will speak of transubstantiation only in the case where the one who expresses himself in the gift of bread and wine is the God-man, it is clear from his explanation that the saving will of God is made relevant to the bread and wine simply through the human symbol-making of Christ. Here the level of God's creative action, however it may be conceived, has certainly not been reached. And the reading of God's saving design in the sacraments is something logically subsequent to his creative-changing action.

The fact that the new theory has been warmly welcomed by not a few Christans who think about their faith and who are attempting to understand the sacraments in personalistic fashion would seem to indicate that the theory possesses positive values. Particularly if the theology of the sacraments is situated in the context of a theology of the word (so that the personalistic character of the sacraments comes to the foreground) it is without doubt valuable to think of God's saving design, his redemptive love, becoming incarnate in the symbol-making of Christ and of his minister. For this reason I am convinced that a large part of Fr. Smits' exposition might very well serve as a personalistic cadre within which a realist theology of the Eucharist could be elaborated.

There are, however, two ways in which I consider his position must be completed. In drawing attention to these it may be possible to meet the objection that the new theory should be criticized from within its own system. I am unrepentant about appealing to the ontological dimension of reality revealed by common sense, for every philosophical system must submit to this judgment—which is not, therefore, external to a system but rather presupposed by every system. However, as the following sections will attempt to show, the new theory also reveals inadequacies precisely as a system applied to the interpretation of the faith.

But if my line of argument will be that one who asserts that he is a convinced phenomenologist cannot account for all the data of revelation, I hope that at the same time it will be possible to give some indications concerning the fashion in which phenomenological insights may be integrated into a realist theology.

THE PROBLEM OF INTEGRATION: REAL PRESENCE

Firstly, it is not at all clear that Fr. Smits has succeeded in distinguishing adequately the Eucharist from the other sacraments or even from the ministry of the word. It would appear that, on his own terms, he ought to admit that all symbol-activity of the Church in which Christ is made present (the sacraments and the word) makes incarnate the saving design of God in broadly the same way as in the Eucharist.

Possibly only in the Eucharist is there a total self-giving of Christ to men; but in the phenomenological theory, so far as I can see, this is only a question of degree. It is far from evident that the fact that Christ gives himself totally in the Eucharist is sufficient to warrant the affirmation that here, and nowhere else in the Church, we have a "substantial presence" of Christ.

The fact is that, in their legitimate desire to underline the reason *why* Christ has given us the Eucharist, the phenomenological theologians have passed over the question of *how* he is present. They do not explain how the Eucharist procures the supreme presence of Christ in his Church, a presence through which our human encounter with our Savior tends towards the integrally human encounter of the Second Coming.

The phenomenological analysis of gift-giving (or violin-playing) itself points to a weakness in the corresponding Eucharistic theory. For, in one way or another, the gift or meal or whatever else it may be *presupposes* either here or elsewhere in the world of experience, the corporeal presence of the donor. This analysis might conceivably be applicable to Christ's offering to his apostles at the Last Supper (though I do not think it is); there, at least, he was corporeally present. In the Church this is precisely what is missing. How can the bread and the wine become extensions of Christ's corporeity when Christ in his corporeity does not fall within our experience?

The problem of the Eucharist is to account for the presence of a person who is otherwise corporeally absent. Physical presence by means of the Eucharist is excluded; the presence we believe in can be achieved only through the medium of a sign-action—the action of gift-giving or meal-offering, let us grant for the moment. Now, however much we may try to escape from a narrow "Western" concept of sign, however much we may attempt to think ourselves into the phenomenological point of view, the fact remains that, in any view, the gift is not the donor. And, whereas a friend's gift may incarnate his friendship, I am able to communicate with him in fully human fashion only if I can achieve direct corporeal contact with him personally.

In the case of Christ, the Eucharist cannot procure such direct corporeal contact. But at least it approaches it; at least it transcends the order of mere gift-action. This is precisely the mystery of the Eucharist; that it transcends the presence-of-Christ-in-his-gift which is characteristic of the whole Church. It gives more: Christ himself. Undeniably, this something more that is given remains contained in the form of a gift of Christ. Yet within this gift the heart of all giving, the self-giving of the donor himself, is realized in a fashion which no mere gift can achieve.

The personal values exhibited in the phenomenological approach must be integrated into a more penetrating philosophy of being if the reality of Christ's presence is not to be falsified. A philosophy of being has its own difficulties with the mystery of the Eucharist; but at least it is searching in the right direction.

One difficulty, raised by proponents of the new theory, may be allayed here. Acceptance of a philosophy of being does not involve the affirmation that bread is a single substance. It appears certain that bread is a conglomeration of several substances. How many, or which are the basic substances in a wafer of bread: these are questions of no interest to a theologian.

It is the fact that there are substances which matters to him—things, that is, enjoying a particular form of existence independently of man. If the Council of Trent spoke, following the fashion of the Middle Ages, of "the substance" of bread, in the singular, there is no difficulty. It was the substantial presence of Christ that the Fathers wished to affirm; this was their teaching on the meaning of Christ's words at the Last Supper. To ensure the reality of this presence they considered it necessary to affirm that only the appearances of bread remain, whatever intimate reality it possessed being replaced by the body of Christ.

What is of primary importance here is the implied affirmation of the *absence* of any substance other than Christ's body. It is this *negative* statement (with its positive accompaniment) which must be maintained, whatever developments there have been in our understanding of the ontological constitution of bread, consequent on the reports of the experimental sciences. If scientific evidence suggests to the metaphysician that bread is a grouping of elemental substances, then it is these which are changed into the body of Christ. This does not involve a multiplicity of presences in the same host; for Christ simply stated: *this* is my body.

The difficulties attendant upon the "realist" understanding of the real presence, when theologically developed, may well have distracted the attention of theologians from adequate development of the reason for the real presence. Here the phenomenological approach can repair omissions. But the basis for everything that can be said about the Eucharist cannot be renounced.

THE PROBLEM OF INTEGRATION: SACRIFICE

There is a second way in which, I consider, the new theory must be completed. While the first proposal was based on a criticism of exclusive reliance on the phenomenological approach, this second one proposes initially a more thorough use of the approach itself.

The whole concern of Fr. Smits and his associates is the

inter-personality of the Eucharist: Christ is made present for men. As a preliminary analysis of Communion no fault can be found with this. But where does the Eucharistic sacrifice appear in this approach?

It is here, I feel, that the weakest point in the new theory is to be discovered, even when it is viewed exclusively from within its own terms of reference. Fr. Smits simply omits reference to the sacrifice in the book under discussion. What the book does contain suggests that he might agree with the explanation of the sacrifice proposed by another contemporary writer. [9]

According to this view, Christ is in the Eucharist as being offered to men; and this in itself is his offering to the Father since he gives himself to men in obedience to the Father, his offering being continued as men unite themselves with it.

If the Eucharist is considered simply as the incarnation of God's friendship for man, such a concept of the sacrifice is a logical conclusion. It seems doubtful whether many theologians will be ready to follow the existentialist definition of Christ as "the man for others" to the point where even his sacrifice is interpreted in exclusively immanent, humanistic terms. It is surely the message of Christianity that it was through total dedication to a transcendent God, to whom alone sacrifice may be offered, that Christ came to the aid of his fellow-men.

This is the startling omission in the new theory. In the offering of the Eucharistic food to men Christ is certainly establishing an inter-personal relation with them. But this inter-personality of the Eucharist is conditioned by the historical mysteries of Christ which are here re-presented sacra-

---

9. A. Winklhofer, "Eucharistie als Opfer, Speise und Anbetung," in *Aktuelle Fragen zur Eucharistie*, ed. M. Schmaus, Munich, 1960, pp. 92-109; cf. pp. 98-99.

mentally. To describe the relationship of God and man in Christ as simply one of friendship is to pass over in silence something essential, namely. the concrete, historical situation in which this friendship was established in Christ.

It was by taking his place among sinners and accepting the consequences of their sin that Christ made friendship between God and man possible. The love of God for man became incarnate in the Christ who died for sin. A sacrifice is the place where we encounter God in Christ. This is the historical shape and the transcendent meaning of the event of Calvary; and this is found in the Eucharist, represented sacramentally.

It is for this reason that I think it must be said that the phenomenological analysis of the new theory is inadequate even as a phenomenology of faith. Christ did not simply give himself to us in the sign of friendship, saying: This is myself. In the situation of the Last Supper, and in the Mass, his concern is not simply to extend his corporeity in a gift of friendship.

Let us consider the event in the Supper room in the phenomenological manner in so far as this is compatible with the postulates of faith. And let it be admitted that when Christ offered the bread and wine he meant by his words: This is myself. This action, undoubtedly expressing friendship, cannot be abstracted from the existential situation of Christ at the Last Supper.

He had made his decision to follow the call of the Father, to set out on his Exodus from the world of sin to the Father; and he was aware that the way of this Exodus lay through his own death. When he presented the bread and wine to his apostles, saying: This is myself, he referred to himself precisely as passing through death and so winning life for all who believe in him. "This is my blood which shall be shed for you." The sacramental presence of Christ bears a reference to the Christ-passing-through-death-to-the-Father.

This points to a unique element in Christ's manner of presence. For, in instituting the Eucharist, Christ was proclaiming his death and yet also his resurrection and the saving significance of his death. He reveals to those who believe in him that his being-in-the-world and his being-with-his-brethren, though they are to be renounced, are, nevertheless, against all expectation, to be restored in a new way which will at once take account of his death and his resurrection.

It appears straightaway that the problem of the Eucharist is drastically over-simplified if it is stated in terms of Christ's being-in-the-world, extending his humanity through gifts. The problem concerns one who, precisely because he has died, is not in the world of experience and yet acquires a totally new kind of corporeal relationship with his disciples.

The problem is misstated if, surreptitiously, Christ's corporeity, his being-with-men, is introduced as given *before* the Eucharist is consecrated; and this is the case when the gift analogy is used. Christ's corporeal presence as preliminary to the Eucharist is precisely what is *not* given in the Church; and a phenomenologist should be the first to remark on this.

The problem is placed correctly only if it is realized that the presence of Christ is an *ecclesial* one and if all the consequences of this are taken into account.

Because it is an ecclesial presence it is situated between the Resurrection and the Parousia, and its purpose is to draw the members of Christ on earth into the saving mysteries of Christ. It communicates the life of Christ and, at the same time, permits the members to participate in the sacrifice of Christ. It is a presence of the risen Christ adapted to those who are not risen, those in whom the mysteries of the death-resurrection are still to be fully realized.

Because it is an ecclesial presence it is a sacramental presence, one, that is, which is mediated through (efficacious) symbols. And it is just this which permits Christ to be present as risen and yet to make himself available to the faithful in a manner adapted to the stage which they have reached in the mystery. His living presence is mediated to them through the placing of the unique *victim* on the altar.

The situation here is far too complicated to be viewed as a gift-giving by Christ or as a simple being-with-men realized in food and drink. Christ's Eucharistic being-with-men is also such that his unique act of renunciation of corporeal being-in-the-world becomes existentially relevant for the Church. By "existentially relevant" is meant that what Christ's death meant as a personal event for Christ, the Eucharistic sacrifice means for the Church. Christ's supreme affirmation of the transcendence of God becomes something in which the Church can, and must, share, and this not simply by faith but further by adopting as her own the victim of Calvary made sacramentally present on her altar. What Christ did on Calvary, the Church participates in—sacramentally—in the Mass.

The model for this mystery is not the exchange of gifts between two persons. Here it is the *unity* of the mystical Christ, head and members, which is given visible, mysterious expression. The gift that Christ gives is himself in the shape of victim so that at the moment of sacrifice the Church is confronted with Christ in the same way that he was confronted with himself when he accepted death. The line of thought is an application to the Eucharist of Romans, ch. 6, where baptism is seen as a sacramental dying in Christ.

In phenomenological terms, there must have been a certain duality in Christ as he accepted his death. That is to say, in affirming the transcendence of his Father, he was also affirming the transcendence of the human person over corporeal being-in-the-world. He was making-himself-distant from his corporeity, the medium through which he belonged to the world. The bread and wine that he blessed and gave to his disciples set himself forth in precisely this condition.

What he meant was not just an embodiment of himself in the gift of food. No; he was already present as a person among his friends and he made himself present in another way: under the appearances of bread and wine, but in reality as the victim of sacrifice. His embodiment of himself transposed himself from a mere friend into what he himself offered as a sacrificial victim. This was the only sacrament Christ himself used; and this precisely because for *this* sacrament a new form of presence had to be given to himself: the form of victim—a form which he did not possess as he spoke with his disciples at the supper-table.

That the living Christ could, and that the risen Christ can, present himself to his members in the form of victim is due to sacramentalism. The apostles and the Church have set before them a symbol of the Christ-Victim; and the symbol mediates the presence of Christ, so that for the apostles and for the Church the existential meaning of the sacramental presence of Christ is that they can offer it. The symbolism is relevant for the members, permitting them to enter the unique sacrifice which is Christ's.

But there would be no true sacrifice for the Church if her victim were merely a symbol. The reality of what lies on the altar must *be* Christ the victim. The offered Christ, as distinct from the offering Christ, must be made available to the Church. In the Eucharist these two aspects are clearly distinguished, as at the supper-table; Christ offers through his minister; Christ is the victim offered. And though, beyond any doubt, it is the risen Christ who is present on the altar, nevertheless he presents himself to the Church according to the need of the Church. In the context of the Church's liturgical sacrifice he is attained as victim. This is the mystery of the Mass: that Christ, personally present, also objectivizes himself for the Church, as he did for himself and his disciples at the Supper.

And just as much as the victim of Calvary belongs to the order of historical events, independently of my grasping its significance for me, the victim of the Mass is an objective reality. I may, indeed, either accept or reject its existential meaning for me; but I could attach no existential significance to it (unless by pure faith) if it were not given, independently of me, as Christ-in-the-state-of-victim, just as Calvary is given.

Now this presents a situation which calls for a radical modification of the phenomenological analysis of the Eucharist which, up to the present, we have been offered by the theologians concerned. Within the person-to-person relationship with God and with Christ established in the Eucharist place must be found for the existential union of the Church with Christ's sacrifice. In this way we return, ultimately, to the common-sense idea of transubstantiation. The reality of what lies on the altar must *be* Christ, the victim. If it is not, there is no sacrifice in the Church.

It will not do to claim that the bread and wine are human extensions of Christ's corporeity in which his friendship is incarnate. There is more than friendship here. There is the friendship of the head of the body who associates his members in his own sacrifice. This demands a new form of being-in-the-world for the risen Christ. He whose glorified body does not fall within our experience gives himself bodily presence among us in the form of a victim by entering the reality of our world, transubstantiating bread and wine, our food.

It should be repeated that this proposal regarding the sacrificial character of the Mass is intended to complement the personalist approach of the new theory. If it radically modifies the theory—and it does—it does not reject its basic personalist insight. For, if the mystery of the Eucharist is more profound than the new theory would lead one to suspect, it remains true that Christ comes to be enthroned, not in the host, but in men's hearts. Add only: being enthroned in men's hearts, he gives himself as victim to be offered by his members.

CONCLUSION

It is necessary, I submit, to reform fundamentally the new theory of transubstantiation, and this by the re-introduction of that ontological dimension which phenomenology, when it remains true to its principles, systematically ignores or "places within brackets." I have argued that this is demanded by the common-sense interpretation which the Church places on the words of institution, but also by the doctrines of creation and of the sacrificial character of the Mass.

I am prepared to go further and to suggest that the new theory, for all its personalistic values, rests on a basic misunderstanding of what sacraments are. It is based on an analysis of Christ-acting-in-the-Church-through-symbols. I have already argued that, in taking for granted the presence of Christ, this conceals an assumption wholly illegitimate for anyone professing phenomenological principles. But, as well, it represents a false and sterile theological approach to the sacraments. For these are not actions initiated by Christ in the liturgical assembly. On the contrary, as is patent, they are symbol-actions of the men and women living in the Church who through them express their faith in the saving mysteries of Christ. The fact that Christ himself enters the major symbol-actions of the Church is logically *subsequent* to this and takes place at another level of reality, the ontological level.

This much more nuanced view of sacramentalism is what is implied by defining sacraments as signs, not as causes. And exploitation of this definition represents the fundamental acquisition of contemporary sacramentology. Curiously, in the face of this renewal, the phenomenological theologians have chosen to apply their analysis to the second, transcendent moment of the sacraments: Christ's hidden entry into the Church's liturgical symbol-actions. This is just the aspect of the sacraments that escapes from normal phenomenology. The most obvious field for such an analysis, where it is valid and valuable, corresponds to the fundamental, human moment of the sacraments. By fidelity to their own principles the phenomenologists would also achieve a more theological view of the sacraments.

The sacraments are the symbol-actions of the Church; that Christ is present in them is a breaking-in of the other world into our world, a development of God's saving action in Christ. But this we can only affirm on faith. It means that our symbol-actions have ceased to be merely things belonging to men.

Should we attempt to project onto the sacramental presence of Christ (the transcendent moment in the sacraments) the phenomenology of human encounters, with the intention of thereby underlining the personalistic character of liturgical practice, then we should be very clear about what we are doing. We are in fact presupposing as given, though not experimentally, the presence of Christ in one fashion or another. On this basis we develop a certain kind of phenomenological description which, I am certain, any self-respecting phenomenologist would reject out of hand as simply not phenomenology.

What we must be vigilant about all the time, if we choose to project the phenomenology of human encounters in this way onto the sacramental-Christ-for-us, is that we are dealing with a wholly unique form of encounter. It was for this reason that, in an earlier chapter, we had to keep on qualifying the term "corporeal presence" in order to take account of the sacramental conditions of that presence; we ended up by saying that there is no solution but to add always the qualification "sacramental."

Where this method of "phenomenological projection" would become theologically indefensible would be if we were to think our phenomenological description could account for the very presupposition which makes our description feasible—namely, the mysterious presence of Christ in our liturgical symbols.